**Sergeant Sandlin:
Kentucky's Forgotten Hero**

**This book was produced
with the assistance
of a grant from**

Sergeant Sandlin

Kentucky's Forgotten Hero

A GIFT TO

_____

FROM

_____

_____, 20 _____

★★★

Book cover design by Adam VanKirk.
The shadow figures behind Willie Sandlin do not represent his World War I contemporaries. Rather they symbolize the millions of American soldiers who came behind Sandlin in service to their country.

Sergeant Sandlin

Kentucky's Forgotten Hero

Every dollar that comes from the sale of this book goes to support the projects and publications of the Jesse Stuart Foundation, a nonprofit publisher and bookseller headquartered in Ashland, Kentucky.

Sergeant Sandlin
Kentucky's Forgotten Hero

James M. Gifford

JSF
JESSE STUART
FOUNDATION
Ashland, Kentucky
2018

SERGEANT SANDLIN: KENTUCKY'S FORGOTTEN HERO

FIRST EDITION

Copyright © 2018 by Jesse Stuart Foundation

All rights reserved. Printed in the United States of America.
No part of this publication may be reproduced in whole or in part,
including photocopying, recording, or by any information or
retrieval system, without written permission of the publisher.

ISBN: 978-1-938471-67-4

Published by
Jesse Stuart Foundation
4440 13th Street
Ashland, Kentucky 41102
(606) 326-1667
jsfbooks.com

TABLE OF CONTENTS

Preface 11
Introduction 13
Chapter One: Kentucky on the Eve of the Great War 23
Chapter Two: Willie Sandlin, 1890-1917 33
Chapter Three: Willie Receives the Medal of Honor 51
Chapter Four: Marriage, Early Family Life, and the Community 87
Chapter Five: Improving His Eastern Kentucky Homeland 103
Chapter Six: No Veteran's Benefits for an Injured Hero, 1921-1933 115
Chapter Seven: Subsistence Farm Life 145
Chapter Eight: Hyden 167
Chapter Nine: Still Trying for Financial Assistance in the 1930s 179
Chapter Ten: The 1940s: A War Hero's Death 195
Chapter Eleven: A Hero's Legacy 211
Epilogue 233
Acknowledgments 235
Endnotes 239
Chronology 253
Appendices 257
Index 267

Captain Carl Leming served as an aviator in the U. S. Army Air Corps during World War II, 1942-1946.

Daniel C. Gifford, Spec/5 U. S. Army, served in combat with a helicopter unit in Vietnam, 1968-1969.

Marine Sgt. Charles Gilley served on the aircraft carrier, *Coral Sea*, 1953-1956.

DEDICATED TO

CARL LEMING
CHARLES GILLEY
DAN GIFFORD

In the processs of writing about a military hero, I hope I have honored Carl, Charles, Dan, and every other man and woman who has served in America's armed forces.

Carl and Buzzy Leming on their wedding day, November 4, 1944.

The Jesse Stuart Foundation is grateful to Carl and Buzzy Leming for their generous sponsorship of this book. For three decades, the Lemings have promoted the work of the Jesse Stuart Foundation. Through heartfelt interest, support, and involvement they have made great contributions to education in Kentucky and across America.

Theirs not to make reply,
Theirs not to reason why,
Theirs but to do and die . . .

"Charge of the Light Brigade"
Alfred, Lord Tennyson

PREFACE

This is not a textbook, nor is it a book written for scholars. It is a popular history and inspirational biography for my fellow Kentuckians to read and enjoy. My endnotes reveal the primary sources that are the backbone of this study of Willie Sandlin's life. In addition to newspaper articles, government documents, and secondary sources, this book also represents the knowledge I have gained from interviews with Willie Sandlin's daughters, Florence Sandlin Muncy and Leona Sandlin Nichols. Because of the subjective nature of some of my source materials, I do not present this book as a definitive biography, but rather as a point of departure for more thought, more analysis, and more writing about Willie Sandlin, one of Kentucky's forgotten heroes.

In other biographies I have written, I allow the subject to speak for himself. I cannot do that with Willie Sandlin, because his words are rarely available to me. In two years of research, I found only two letters and one postcard written by him. Even when he is quoted in newspaper articles, I am concerned about the accuracy or the intention of the quote. One day, another historian may discover a treasure trove of Sandlin information and some of the questions that have haunted me may be answered. For the present, however, this book can inform general readers and also serve as a resource for other historians who may choose to add Willie Sandlin to the long list of America's exemplary citizen-

SERGEANT SANDLIN

Left: Florence Sandlin Muncy and her son, Jamie Karl "Butch" Asher, August 2016. Sadly, Butch died on May 26, 2017, and did not live to see his grandfather's biography appear in print. *Photo by Adam VanKirk.* Right: Leona Sandlin Nichols in her home with her father's picture in the background. *Photo courtesy of Lue Peabody.*

soldiers or to the distinguished company of Appalachia's military heroes.

More than anything else, Willie Sandlin stands as a symbol for millions of unrecognized veterans, extraordinary people who won wars and, like Sergeant Sandlin, returned home to live responsible and productive lives. We are losing thousands of those veterans every day. The men and women who gave so much and asked so little in return are quietly departing a nation that owes them a debt that can never be repaid. With this book, I salute Willie Sandlin and all other veterans for their service and their sacrifices. I encourage everyone who reads this book to express thanks to a veteran. Sometimes a hug or a handshake means more than a war memorial, a museum exhibit, a written tribute, or a statue.

The tree of liberty must be refreshed from time to time with the blood of patriots and tyrants.

Thomas Jefferson, 1787
Letter to William Stephens Smith

INTRODUCTION: A FORGOTTEN HERO

In 1917, after several years of provocation, America declared war on Germany and, by November of the following year, the United States had sent two million men overseas. In April of 1918, American ground forces played a decisive role in the fighting which broke the Hindenburg Line and forced Germany's eventual surrender.

In the bloody fighting that took place in the Meuse-Argonne Forest in the fall of 1918, thousands of Americans distinguished themselves, including two young men from central Appalachia who received the Medal of Honor. On September 26, 1918, Sergeant Willie Sandlin, acting alone, attacked and disabled three German machine gun

---

Willie Sandlin was extremely shy and modest, but on one occasion he was persuaded to re-enact his heroics of September 26, 2018. *University of Louisville Archives.*

SERGEANT SANDLIN

Willie Sandlin prior to World War I. *Florence Muncy Collection.*

nests and killed all twenty-four occupants. Less than two weeks later, Corporal Alvin York led an attack on a German machine gun nest, taking 35 machine guns, killing at least 25 enemy soldiers, and capturing 132. Sandlin was from Hyden in Leslie County, Kentucky, and York was from a town just across the Kentucky line in Pall Mall, Tennessee. Although York and Sandlin emerged from similar Appalachian communities and shared similar personalities, temperaments, and military distinctions, their lives after World War I were remarkably different. [1] York acquired money and fame and became a national icon and an international celebrity. Sandlin lived in modest circumstances, ill-health, and purposeful obscurity until he died of war-inflicted gas poisoning at age 59.

The above reads:

THIS IS TO CERTIFY THAT
THE PRESIDENT OF THE UNITED STATES OF AMERICA
PURSUANT TO ACT OF CONGRESS APPROVED JULY 9, 1918,
HAS AWARDED IN THE NAME OF CONGRESS TO

Willie Sandlin

THE CONGRESSIONAL MEDAL OF HONOR FOR VALOR
ABOVE AND BEYOND THE CALL OF DUTY IN ACTION INVOLVING
ACTUAL CONFLICT WITH AN ENEMY OF THE UNITED STATES
At Bois de Forges, France, September 26, 1918, while serving as sergeant, Company A, 132nd Infantry, 33rd Division, American Expeditionary Forces.

SERGEANT SANDLIN

America was prepared to honor Sergeant Alvin York when his troopship arrived at New York harbor in May, 1919, because his deeds had been widely publicized. Americans knew his story and they knew the great character of the man who had quickly become a larger-than-life American hero. In New York and Washington, high officials of the army and navy and government, along with civilian leaders, gathered at receptions and banquets in his honor. People lined the streets and pushed against one another to get a glimpse of York. The New York Stock Exchange suspended business when he arrived and members carried him over the floor on their shoulders. In Washington, members of the House of Representatives stopped debate and rose as one to cheer when York arrived in the gallery.

Alvin York, a man with a third-grade education, emerged as the Great War's greatest hero. *National Archives.*

When Willie Sandlin returned from Europe and arrived in New York, he was unknown and unrecognized. A woman named Florence Norwood met and befriended the lonely young soldier and took an interest in his life over the years. Years later Willie Sandlin and his wife Belvia named their youngest daughter Florence Norwood Sandlin.

When Alvin York was mustered out of the service, there were orations for him at various railroad stations. After he left the railroad station nearest his home,

INTRODUCTION: A FORGOTTEN HERO

When Sergeant Willie Sandlin was discharged from service, **he rode the train to Hazard and walked the last ten miles to his home** *near Hyden with a pocket full of medals.*

Sergeant Alvin York was truly a religious man. Beginning on January 1, 1915, York put his rough and rowdy ways behind him and pledged "to live the life God wants me to live." *National Archives.*

he traveled forty-eight miles to his home in Pall Mall. Along the way, people in automobiles, on horseback, on mules, and whole families riding in chairs in the beds of farm wagons turned out to see and honor their hero.

When Willie Sandlin was discharged from service, he rode the train to Hazard and walked the last ten miles to his home near Hyden with a pocket full of medals. Few knew of his remarkable accomplishments and he returned home quietly, without immediate recognition of his heroism.

Because York had become nationally famous, the people of Tennessee began to gather gifts for him even before he left France. Several cities offered him a home with desirable farm land. York, however, wished to live "nowhere but at Pall Mall." Soon an adoring public gave him 400 acres of valuable

17

SERGEANT SANDLIN

farm land and timbered mountain slopes that had originally belonged to his ancestors and later "lost in the vicissitudes of the days following the Civil War."

After Sandlin returned home and married, his father-in-law loaned him money to purchase a farm, but Sandlin was soon forced to sell it because of poor health combined with the financial challenges of the depression. Several groups attempted to raise money to purchase a farm for Sandlin, but he never saw a dollar of the "Hero Fund" or any other fundraising efforts in his name.

> *When Sergeant Alvin York returned home from the war, **he was overwhelmed with business opportunities**, including a guaranteed contract for $75,000 to appear in a moving picture about his life.*

Sergeant York returned home to marry his sweetheart, Miss Gracie Williams on June 7, 1919, at Pall Mall. The ceremony was performed by the Governor of Tennessee. The bridal tour was a welcome-home trip to Nashville, where the state's medal bearing the inscription "Service Above Self" awaited the great hero. York was appointed to the Governor's staff at the rank of Colonel. Alvin's new wife and his mother made a good impression "upon the gorgeous social battalion" in Nashville.

Willie Sandlin came home for six months and then returned to France as a graves checker for the Americans killed in battle there and as an escort for bodies being returned to the United States. Willie came home for good in 1920. On June 4, 1920, he married Belvia Roberts, a woman from a relatively prosperous family in Leslie County.

When York retuned home, he was overwhelmed with business opportunities, including a guaranteed contract for $75,000 to appear in a moving picture about his life that would be staged in the Argonne Forest in France. The wide-ranging offers that included vaudeville and theatrical engagements would have brought York thousands of dollars per week, but "the theatre was condemned by the tenets of his church" and as York declared many

INTRODUCTION: A FORGOTTEN HERO

Alvin York was more than a hero. He was a celebrity, although he did not seek fame. People constantly wanted to shake his hand or to have a photograph made with him. *Library of Congress.*

times, "Uncle Sam's uniform ain't for sale."[2] Yet every day the postman arrived by horseback with several mail pouches filled with an overwhelming range of correspondence. Some were from people who wanted to help him, and some were from people asking for help and/or advice. Also included among these letters were belated matrimonial proposals. Sandlin received one or two offers about books and movies, but he ignored them completely.

Both men used their fame to improve the quality of life in their Appalachian homelands. York received monetary gifts to support his efforts while Sandlin donated his time on an in-kind basis.

In 1941, at the beginning of World War II, York was glorified in a major

Late in life, Alvin York suffered financial difficulties that prompted a national fundraising campaign. On The Ed Sullivan Show on CBS, Sullivan asked the American people to help York. He concluded

> *If all of you throughout the country agree with me that this is a cruel, ironic, and heartbreaking thing to happen to one of America's greatest heroes, won't you sit down with me tonight after our show and send whatever small or large sum of money you can afford to the Sergeant York Fund, Washington, DC. Never let it be said that when the chips were down for Sergeant York, we pulled away from him. Because certainly, with the chips down, he never pulled away from us.*

INTRODUCTION: A FORGOTTEN HERO

Sgt. Alvin York remained a national icon and celebrity until his death on September 2, 1964, at the age of 76. In sharp contrast, **poor health and financial difficulties constantly plagued Sandlin after the Great War ended, and he died on May 29, 1949, at the age of 59**, *from exposure to the poison gas the German army used in battle.*

motion picture starring Gary Cooper, and "he became a hero all over again." Sadly, the $150,000 that York received from the movie about his life led to problems with the IRS. In 1959, he supported himself, his wife, and an elderly sister-in-law on less than $4,000 per year and had debts of more than $200,000, including $172,723.60 that he owed to the IRS. With the help of Speaker of the House Sam Rayburn and Tennessee Congressman Joe Evans, York's tax problems were mediated, while a national fund-raising effort on his behalf brought modest financial security to his remaining years. [3] He remained a national icon and celebrity until his death on September 2, 1964, at the age of 76. In sharp contrast, poor health and financial difficulties constantly plagued Sandlin after the Great War ended, and he died on May 29, 1949, at the age of 59, from exposure to the poison gas the German army used in battle.

What follows is the never-before-told life story of Willie Sandlin, a painfully shy, country boy raised in Appalachian poverty. Because Sandlin left no written records and because he refused radio interviews, biographical accounts, or movies of his life, he has faded into historical obscurity. Here, on the 100th anniversary of his Medal of Honor heroism, is the story of Willie Sandlin, one of Kentucky's forgotten heroes.

This cartoon advocates "strict neutrality." The United States could not stand for peace, some argued, while helping other nations fight. *Library of Congress.*

The color of the ground was in him, the red earth;
The smack and tang of elemental things.

"Lincoln, the Man of the People"
Edwin Markham

CHAPTER ONE
KENTUCKY ON THE EVE OF THE GREAT WAR

In 1900, Kentucky transitioned from an unhappy past to a troubled future. Outsiders saw Kentucky as a "dark and bloody ground" where nineteenth century feuds were followed by the assassination of Governor William Goebel on January 30, 1900. In 1900, Kentucky was clearly a rural state. Approximately 80% of the population was poor and rural, and of the 20% of the population that was urban, most lived in or near Louisville. At the turn of the century, the state contained almost 250,000 farms smaller than one hundred acres. [1]

For rural Kentuckians, life centered around small, but important, institutions: the country store, the rural church, the one-room school, and the village post office. In a still violent land that counted at least 10% of its residents as illiterate, state Superintendent of Public Instruction John G. Crabbe introduced the Sullivan Law of 1908 which completely reorganized Kentucky's public school system and created a tax base to support the schools. Meanwhile the state was developing a professional corps of teachers at teacher training schools in Morehead, Richmond, Bowling Green, and Lexington. Still by 1918, almost 200,000 school-age children were not enrolled in classes. Kentucky was also in the process of developing a better system of roads when a European war began in 1914 that would soon involve the United States. [2]

The world war, which began in August 1914 when a Serbian assassinated the heir to the throne of Austria-Hungary, ended a century of relative peace. Soon Europe was polarized into two relatively equal warring alliances. It was a war between the tiger and the shark. One was the land power of Germany and Austria-Hungary. The other was the sea power of Britain, France, and Russia.

> *The world war, which began in August 1914 when a Serbian assassinated the heir to the throne of Austria-Hungary, ended a century of relative peace. Soon **Europe was polarized into two relatively equal warring alliances**.*

From the very beginning of the European war, most Americans believed their country should (and could) remain neutral. Yet it was almost impossible to follow President Woodrow Wilson's advice that America remain neutral in thought and deed. Because we were a nation descended from the British Isles, support for the Allied Powers was great. However, many poor Americans still saw England as a land of powerful aristocrats and they did not support Great Britain and France, and, of course, there was a large German minority in the U.S. that enthusiastically favored their Fatherland. When the war began, America took the position – supported by law and precedent – that all belligerent nations were free to purchase supplies from the United States. However, British naval power made this almost impossible because the British blockaded Europe and stopped American cargo ships that would have delivered supplies to Germany. By 1915, the American economy – that had been entering a depression one year earlier – was booming. Into this conflict, Germany introduced a new weapon – the submarine – designed to break the British blockade of Europe. Still America tried to remain neutral, but when Germany

American hopes for continued neutrality suffered a severe setback in early 1915. The Germans announced their U-boats would attack merchant ships in British waters, even those flying neutral flags. The unprovoked attack on the *Lusitania* horrified the people of America, but most still hoped to keep out of war. *Library of Congress.*

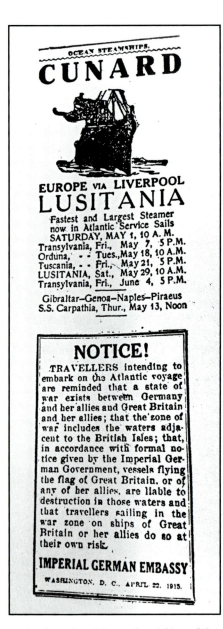

Lusitania notice. Prior to the sinking of the Lusitania, the German embassy published the above warning in New York papers. Library of Congress.

began sinking supply ships and passenger liners, American sentiment moved even more strongly in favor of the Allies.

The U-boats, as the German submarines were called, focused only on attacking warships until 1915, when the German Emperor announced that all the waters around the British Isles constituted a war zone and that any merchant ship attempting to trade with the Allies would be destroyed. While America attempted neutrality, they suffered losses from both sides. The British were seizing American cargoes bound for Europe; even more disturbing, the German U-boats had killed almost 200 Americans. On February 10, 1915, President Wilson informed the German government that the U.S. government would hold Germany to "a strict accountability for property damaged or lives lost." On May 1, 1915, a German submarine sank the *Lusitania*, a British passenger liner, off the coast of Ireland. Of the 1100 lives lost, 128 were Americans, including some women. The Germans had torpedoed the ship without warning and made no effort to rescue passengers. American diplomats desperately sought an apology and reparations, but war with Germany seemed inevitable.

KENTUCKY AND THE GREAT WAR

WORLD WAR I ON THE HOME FRONT

A THOMAS D. CLARK MEDALLION BOOK

DAVID J. BETTEZ

David Bettez' award-winning book, *Kentucky and The Great War*, is a must-read for those who wish to understand Sandlin's life in a broader context.
It is a masterful analysis of the impact of the First World War on Kentucky's politics, economy, and culture. Bettez shows that Kentuckians put aside party politics and worked together to help the nation achieve victory in Europe.
Photo courtesy of The University Press of Kentucky.

Councils of Defense

Fearing that America would be drawn into the European war, President Wilson wisely, but reluctantly, began preparations for American involvement. Late in 1916, Wilson created a Council of National Defense (CND) to develop economic plans for the war. Six cabinet members served on the CND. They enjoyed the support of a seven-person Advisory Commission of prominent leaders from the private sector. [3]

As the CND began planning and gathering data, the chair, Secretary of War Newton Baker, "encouraged all governors to create state councils of defense." Consequently, Kentucky Governor Augustus O. Stanly appointed a State Council of Defense. In May 1917, almost fifty of Kentucky's leaders met in Lexington to discuss Kentucky's major contributions: Liberty Bonds, draft registrations, and agricultural products. Several eastern Kentucky leaders played a significant role in Kentucky's Council of Defense (KCD), including George B. Martin of Catlettsburg; William Duffield, from Mason County; and West Liberty doctor, S. R. Collier. [4]

Following the national model, the KCD created county councils of defense (CDC) patterned after the state council. The county councils were often energetically active. They helped to register men for the draft and advised local men about military experience. Later the county committees helped draftees "in managing the details of their private business" while many of them were fighting in Europe. Representatives of the county committees made public presentations

> *County councils of Kentucky's Council of Defense* **helped to register men for the draft and advised local men about military experience.** *Later the county committees helped draftees "in managing the details of their private business" while many of them were fighting in Europe.*

Sixty-fifth Congress of the United States of America;

At the First Session,

Begun and held at the City of Washington on Monday, the second day of April, one thousand nine hundred and seventeen.

JOINT RESOLUTION

Declaring that a state of war exists between the Imperial German Government and the Government and the people of the United States and making provision to prosecute the same.

Whereas the Imperial German Government has committed repeated acts of war against the Government and the people of the United States of America: Therefore be it

Resolved by the Senate and House of Representatives of the United States of America in Congress assembled, That the state of war between the United States and the Imperial German Government which has thus been thrust upon the United States is hereby formally declared; and that the President be, and he is hereby, authorized and directed to employ the entire naval and military forces of the United States and the resources of the Government to carry on war against the Imperial German Government; and to bring the conflict to a successful termination all of the resources of the country are hereby pledged by the Congress of the United States.

Champ Clark,
Speaker of the House of Representatives.

Tho. R. Marshall
Vice President of the United States and
President of the Senate.

Approved 6 April, 1917.
Woodrow Wilson

A declaration of war, pledging all U.S. resources to the war, was passed and approved by Congress on April 6, 1917. *National Archives.*

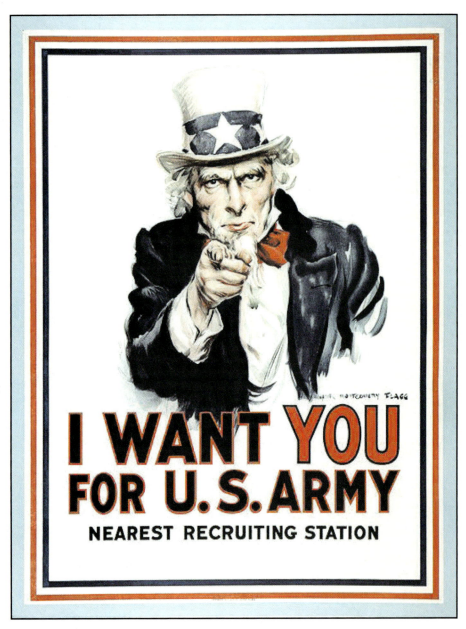

American artist James Montgomery Flagg, 1877-1940, created the iconic "I Want You" recruiting and enlistment poster in 1917. Within a month of America's declaration of war, approximately 10 million men in the 21-30 age group had registered. *Library of Congress.*

encouraging everyone to support America's war effort, reminding their friends and neighbors that it was "not only going to take bullets but bread to win the great battle that is now being waged." Perhaps the CDC inspired patriotic enthusiasm in Hyden, Willie's hometown, during the war. In the June 1918 Red Cross war fund, Hyden, "which had no chapter and no quota, raised $2000." [5]

Later, as the war drew to a close, county councils helped returning servicemen adjust to civilian life and aided them in gaining or regaining employment. Significantly, for later historians, the county councils were also charged with keeping a record of "the history of Kentucky's part in the World War." Many years later these county histories would provide the basic details, at the local level, of Kentucky's involvement in the Great War. [6]

America Joins the War

Despite American diplomatic efforts to remain neutral, the United States was slowly drawn into the European war. President Woodrow Wilson tried to avoid American involvement and privately stated that God would hold him personally responsible for American deaths if the United States entered the war, but finally, on April 2, 1917, Wilson delivered his war message to a solemn Congress. In ringing, eloquent words, Wilson denounced Germany's submarine warfare against "the lives of peaceful and innocent people" and called upon Americans to rise in a great crusade to make the world "safe for democracy." Four days later, on April 6, 1917, the United States declared war against Germany. The following month Congress adopted a Selective Service Act to register American men between the ages of twenty-one and thirty. By the end of "the Great War," twenty-four million men had registered and almost five million American men had served, including Willie Sandlin, born in Breathitt County, Kentucky. Sandlin enlisted at age 23 in Jackson, Breathitt County, April 16, 1913. [7]

The only extant photo of Willie Sandlin's parents, John Sandlin and Lucinda Abner Sandlin. For more information on Willie's immediate family, see the chart on page 34. *Florence Muncy Collection.*

My heart tells me to fight to end this war
And live these things I think I'm fighting for.

Kentucky Is My Land
Jesse Stuart

CHAPTER TWO
WILLIE SANDLIN, 1890-1917

If war is a rich man's war and a poor man's fight, then Willie Sandlin [1] represented millions of poor men who became soldiers during World War I. Born into Appalachian poverty on January 1, 1890, on Long's Creek in Breathitt County, Kentucky, Sandlin's parents were John "Dirty Face" Sandlin (born March 17, 1867) and Lucinda Abner Sandlin (born December 12, 1870). John and Lucinda had five sons: Charlie, Willie, John, Elihu (Sonny), and Mathew (Mathy). Willie was their second son. His mother was from Dalesboro, a small community at the head of Freeman Fork on the Perry, Breathitt, and Leslie County border. People who knew Willie said that he favored his mother's people, the Abners. He was 5'7" tall and "straight as an arrow" with keen, alert black eyes and black hair. He was, in the parlance of his people, "country strong" but slender, a prototype of Kentucky's sturdy, mountain youth. Willie's mother and father divorced in 1900. [2]

When Willie was a boy, his father was imprisoned in Perry County for the lynching murder of an African-American man, Henderson Barger. According to Breathitt County historian Stephen Bowling, "It was not primarily a race-related murder. Sandlin along with other coal miners in the area were concerned that African-American and Hungarian immigrants were taking their jobs." The

Willie Sandlin's birth certificate. John and Lucinda had five children – all sons. Willie was the second oldest. He was born January 1, 1890.

WILLIE SANDLIN, 1890-1917

*During the years when Willie and his siblings lived with their mother, **they did not have shoes and they often went to bed hungry**. When snow covered the ground, the impoverished, barefoot children used two boards to get from their house to the outhouse.*

---

murder, according to Bowling, was primarily a labor issue, and John played an accessory role. [3] The crime took place in Perry County, and Sandlin and two other men were arrested there. The case was transferred to the Harlan Circuit Court from the Perry County Court in April 1898. John Sandlin was found guilty in a jury trial on April 28, 1898, and sentenced to serve a life term in the state penitentiary in Frankfort. Sandlin then appealed this verdict to the State Court of Appeals. He was transferred to the Lincoln County jail while the verdict was under appeal, because there was "a strong possibility that an attempt to rescue them" was going to be made by their friends if they were "left in jail in Harlan County." [4] After John Sandlin was paroled from prison in 1908, he deserted his family, left Kentucky, and started another family.

During the years when Willie and his siblings lived with their mother, they did not have shoes and they often went to bed hungry. When snow covered the ground, the impoverished, barefoot children used two boards to get from their house to the outhouse. They laid down one board and carried the other. When they got to the end of the board on the ground, they laid down the one in their hands, stepped forward on it, and reached back to pick up the first board. In this way, they progressed to the outhouse and back without walking barefoot through the snow. Like many poor children in Appalachia, Willie was not forced to attend school "but allowed to remain at home if he desired." In later years, he realized that as a child, between the ages of seven and ten, "he did not realize the value of an education." [5]

> ## Willie's Parents
>
> **John Sandlin** (March 17, 1867 - February 3, 1947)
> **Lucinda Abner** (December 12, 1870 - August 8, 1900)
> Married 1885, Divorced 1900
>
> Their children:
> Charlie Sandlin (November 25, 1888 - October 19, 1950)
> Willie Sandlin (January 1, 1890 - May 29, 1949)
> John Sandlin (August 11, 1892 - November 19, 1972)
> Elihu Sandlin (March 10, 1895 - May 25, 1928)
> Mathew Sandlin (December 15, 1896 - November 3, 1987)
>
> John Sandlin, after getting out of jail and moving out of the state, had other children who are Willie's half-siblings. They are not listed here.

Lucinda, who was half Native American, died in child birth in 1900, so Willie and his motherless siblings were divided among relatives, as was the custom of the day. According to family lore, Willie was outside milking a cow, desperate for something to sustain his ailing mother, when he looked up and saw an apparition of his mother standing near him. When Willie went into his house, he found that his mother had just died. According to his family, Willie was able to see ghosts and spirits throughout his life. Willie's brothers Elihu and Mathew remained on Long's Creek where they were raised by their mother's sister, Eliza Baker, and her husband, James Todd Baker. Willie and his brothers Charlie and John were raised by his father's relatives on Hell-for-Certain Creek in Leslie County. However, Willie, Charlie, and John often returned to Breathitt

WILLIE SANDLIN, 1890-1917

County to visit with their two younger brothers. According to his daughter, Florence Muncy, Willie was raised by Allan Muncy and he may have also received some assistance from Bill Abner of Perry County. Allan Muncy was a farmer with children of his own, but he added Willie to his family and loved him like a son. Those feelings were mutual. Willie loved Allan and his wife like parents, and he loved their children like they were his brothers and sisters. He was especially close to Vidge Muncy, who was close to his own age. The boys hunted and fished together. After the war ended, Vidge moved to North Carolina, where Willie visited him for hunting and fishing trips that strengthened their boyhood ties. [6]

> **Willie Sandlin had four brothers in the war;** one was wounded seven times and two others remained in the service after the armistice.

The late Joe Hart, a *Courier-Journal* journalist for many years, grew up with Willie and also served with him in 1914, when Willie was soldiering in Texas with the Eleventh Infantry. Hart remembered that young Willie and another boy visited his home, and they hunted and hiked together. On one occasion, "Willie showed us how to make a whale of a 'gun' by letting water trickle on substantial glowing coals and giving the steaming mass a sharp blow with the poll of an ax." As a boy, Sandlin was good natured and seldom fought, but "somehow it got around that it was a pretty good policy to respect him." Several years later, Sandlin got in a scrap with six rivermen at Athol, Kentucky. The men were "heavily armed and in a fighting mood" but left quickly when they found a revolver pointed at them. [7] Willie and his siblings grew up quickly and became self-sufficient at an early age. Willie had little formal education, but after he reached enlistment age, he and his brothers joined the regular army. Sandlin had four brothers in the war; one was wounded seven times and two others remained in the service after the armistice. [8] Between 1913 and 1919, Willie Sandlin would serve under General John J. Pershing on two continents, and he would receive his nation's highest military

Willie Sandlin, age 23, enlisted in the army on April 16, 1913. He enlisted in Jackson, the county seat of Breathitt County and served on the Mexican border before the United States entered World War I. *Florence Muncy Collection.*

honor, the Medal of Honor, for exemplary heroism against the German army on September 26, 1918.

While Willie Sandlin and thousands of other eastern Kentucky soldiers were fighting the German army in Europe, their friends and family at home lashed out against all things German. A German language newspaper in Kentucky offered the following advice to German-Americans:

> *Our condition will be very unpleasant. We will be watched with suspicious eyes and we will be charged with the most disgraceful plans. This attitude we can only combat with caution, and by avoiding everything which might give the least offense. Protest and indignation meetings must absolutely cease. All outburst of anger must be avoided. We must follow the motto of the suffering Kaiser, 'Learn to suffer without complaint.' Whether we will or no, we must do our duty as American citizens. We owe it to the oath of allegiance which we took to the Union, we owe it to our families.*

Into this anti-German hysteria, Kentucky officials were urged "to use any means to prevent acts of violence" against German-Americans in Kentucky. On April 9, 1917, U.S. District Attorney Thomas O. Slattery of Covington received the following policy statement from the Department of Justice in Washington:

> *No German alien enemy in this country who has not hitherto been implicated in plots against the interests of the U.S. need have any fear of actions by the Department of Justice so long as he observes the following warning: "Obey the law; keep your mouth shut."* [9]

But government dictates cannot control public emotions, and people of

War hysteria led to vigilante action in many places. Many German-Americans were jailed; some were tarred and feathered; a few were lynched. *National Archives.*

Federal courts were of little value in protecting the civil liberties of Americans who were suspected of being pro-German. Many Americans suffered as a result of false atrocity stories and irresponsible propaganda. In the Ohio statehouse in Columbus, pictures of prominent German-Americans were turned to the wall. Semiofficial vigilantism resulted in a reign of terror in parts of the United States. *National Archives.*

Anti-German hysteria took several forms before and during World War I. In this photo, "enemy aliens" are fingerprinted and registered. *National Archives.*

German ancestry were eyed with suspicion and distrust. Anti-German sentiment found expression in rallies, intimidations, and vigilante violence. In many eastern Kentucky towns, the school systems forbade German-language classes. By 1919, fifteen states had declared it a criminal offense to teach in any language but English, not merely in public schools but private as well. Several institutions and organizations with the word "German" in the title were renamed. Even German-sounding words were altered. For example, Frankfurters became liberty dogs. On one occasion, a Kentucky town name was changed; Himlerville, a coal mining community in Martin County that had been founded by Hungarian immigrants in the early 1900s, was renamed "Beauty" in 1919. Xenophobic emotion was in the saddle and riding hard when the Ashland City Council chose not to renew the business license of the Lexington Brewing Company because it was "managed by an unworthy fellow who boasts of spelling his name 'the Hun way' – Fischer." *The Big Sandy News* in Louisa congratulated this "brave city" for a decision that made "life miserable for everything of a German tendency."[10]

John J. Pershing and the Mexican Border

By 1916, John Joseph Pershing had already established a brilliant military career. Born in 1860, Pershing graduated from West Point where he was elected class president. By 1913, he had fought in the Indian Wars against the Sioux and Apache tribes, the Spanish-American War, and the insurrection in the Philippines. After serving as a military attaché in Tokyo during the Sino-Russian War, Pershing returned to the United States and was nominated as a brigadier general by President Theodore Roosevelt. Greater command responsibilities awaited the man who had earned the sobriquet "Black Jack" Pershing for commanding the all-black 10th Cavalry, but the nickname also signified his stern demeanor and the rigorous discipline he applied to himself and his troops.

Beginning in 1911, political turmoil in Mexico led to recurrent problems along the border between the United States and Mexico. On March 9, 1916, Mexican revolutionary Pancho Villa and 500 to 1000 troops made a surprise attack on Columbus, New Mexico. Villa's troops killed 18 American soldiers and civilians, wounded 20 others, and destroyed a great deal of property before they were driven back into Mexico by the 13th Cavalry. Ignoring international protocols about foreign borders, President Woodrow Wilson ordered Pershing to cross the border

> *On March 9, 1916, Mexican revolutionary Pancho Villa and 500 to 1000 troops made a surprise attack on Columbus, New Mexico.* **Villa's troops killed 18 American soldiers and civilians, wounded 20 others**, *and destroyed a great deal of property before they were driven back into Mexico by the 13th Cavalry.*

SERGEANT SANDLIN

and capture the Mexican bandit. On March 15, Pershing and his Punitive Expedition entered Mexico in "hot pursuit." For almost a year, Pershing's army tracked the elusive desperado through northern Mexico and fought the Mexicans several times, but they never captured Pancho Villa. The Punitive Expedition was a "trying ordeal" for Pershing's soldiers. "Native beef and parched corn" were their principal ration. While they pursued Villa, men "wore out their clothes and shoes and were obliged in many instances to use their shelter tents for patches." Some bound their feet with "their stirrup hoods . . . to keep them from being absolutely barefoot." [11] On January 27, 1917, after nine difficult and unsuccessful months in Mexico, the Punitive Expedition rode back to Texas.

Brigadier General John J. Pershing (above) led a punitive expedition into Mexico that failed to capture Pancho Villa.
National Archives.

Sandlin probably did not cross into Mexico with Pershing's ill-fated punitive expedition. Sandlin was a corporal in Company H of the 35th Infantry, which was organized July 1916 at Nogales, Arizona. Because tensions with Mexico were rising, the 35th Infantry Regiment was formed to provide additional security at the border between Arizona and Mexico. Sandlin was one of the original members of the Regiment. [12] While stationed in Arizona, Sandlin and the soldiers of the 10th Cavalry "had time to reflect on the events in Europe and waited anxiously to learn if they were going to get in on the fighting." However, they also believed that their duty on the border was important, because some American military officials felt that the Arizona border was a place where German agents could inspire an attack by the Mexican army. [13]

Willie Sandlin is promoted to Corporal (top). General John J. Pershing and staff at field headquarters near Casas Grandes, Mexico. Pershing is fourth from the left. Standing behind Pershing's left shoulder is Lieutenant George S. Patton. *Library of Congress.*

Willie Sandlin, May of 1920. *Florence Muncy Collection.*

WILLIE SANDLIN, 1890-1917

Sandlin was in Nogales when his enlistment expired on April 16, 1917. During his time on the border, Sandlin earned a reputation as a peaceable man, but a fierce fighter. One evening, while Willie and Joe Hart soldiered in Texas, they found themselves in the middle of an ongoing conflict between artillerymen and infantrymen. [14] The artillerymen were sometimes called "the jackass artillery" because their guns were hauled by donkeys or mules, and the artillerymen had to lift the heavy guns onto the backs of their pack animals. For that reason, artillerymen were big and strong "in order to help out man's second best friend, the jackass." These men held themselves in high regard as fighting men and wore red cords on their bonnets as a mark of distinction. When they came upon an infantryman with a blue-corded hat, their standard order was, "Get off the sidewalk, punk, and let a man pass."

> *Willie Sandlin was in Nogales when his enlistment expired on April 16, 1917. During his time on the border,* **Sandlin earned a reputation as a peaceable man, but a fierce fighter**.

One night when Willie and his friend Joe Hart were strolling down the streets of Texas City, they encountered three artillerymen – "mean as the devil and twice as tall" – who had been drinking "essence of panther" and had an "artificially exaggerated" sense of their prowess. They delivered their standard ultimatum: "get off the sidewalk and let a man pass." In short order, Willie whipped an artilleryman who had pulled out a pair of "steel knucks." Willie's opponent was soon staggering around in a gutter picking pieces of a glass bottle out of his head. The other two withdrew "in force."

Willie handed Joe the brass knuckles that he took from his adversary and suggested that they leave immediately to avoid the provost guard. In 1949, the year of his friend's death, Joe still had the brass knuckles as a souvenir of his rowdy days and nights on the Mexican border. "By staying with Willie, I found they were never needed," he remembered. [15]

SERGEANT SANDLIN

During the time that Willie served on the Mexican border, Pancho Villa had escaped capture, but American troops benefitted from intensive training for both Regular Army and National Guard troops. The experience on the border made Willie Sandlin a better soldier. He re-enlisted on April 17, 1917, and later that year he was sent to Europe to serve with the American Expeditionary Force (AEF) under Pershing. On the troopships that carried them to Europe, Sandlin and the soldiers of the 33rd Division were "required to keep their clothes on at all times" during the voyage to Europe in order to be prepared "to take to the boats" in the event they were torpedoed by a German submarine.

One soldier wrote: "You should see the way this old ship has been rocking . . . The waves splash clear up on the top deck." Many of the soldiers suffered from seasickness and difficult accommodations. "The beds," observed one soldier, "were made for someone about four feet long and the eats were made for someone besides me. . . . However I manage to get filled up and don't go hungry." The sailors ate at separate tables and had better accommodations than the soldiers, so they brought food to them. The men of the 33rd were looking forward to seeing land again. "The nearest we have been to land is 3 ½ miles, and that is straight down." [16]

In 1917, after America's entry into World War I, General Pershing was appointed commander in chief of the American Expeditionary Force. At that time, the U.S. Army consisted of 130,000 men and no reserves. Eighteen months later, Pershing had transformed the American military into a disciplined army of more than two million men, including Sergeant Willie Sandlin. Pershing may have felt a kinship with Sandlin because the General's mother was of Scots-Irish ancestry and her family had moved from Kentucky to Missouri, where Pershing was born at the beginning of the Civil War. [17] By 1918, Sandlin had been promoted to sergeant in Company A, 132 Infantry, 33rd Division.

Willie Sandlin is promoted to Sergeant.

Given to Sandlin's Division after the war.
(John Trowbridge)

German machine gunners retreating at Belleau Wood. *National World War I Museum and Memorial, Kansas City, Missouri.*

Oh, Jefferson – what you declared in ink
Each hedgerow claimed a thousand times in blood!

"Welcome to Hell"
Phil Hardin

CHAPTER THREE
WILLIE RECEIVES THE MEDAL OF HONOR

When war was declared, Sandlin was offered a commission in the Officers' Reserve Training Corps. He refused it because of his lack of education.[1] In July 1918, the 33rd Division advanced a mile and half against the German Army. They took more than one thousand prisoners and suffered very few casualties. Arthur Beverly, a soldier in the 33rd, wrote that at 3:00 am, just as it was becoming daylight, "we went over the top." They were allied with an Australian unit, and "such princely men you never have seen. They are . . . generous, good-hearted, and well-mannered fellows" and they worked well with the Americans. Their advance against the German army "was a real battle with tanks, aeroplanes, and lots of artillery."[2]

In July of 1918, sensing that the war-weary German army had lost its fighting momentum, the Allies saw an opportunity to deliver the knock-out punch that would end the Great War. Supreme Allied Commander Ferdinand Foch drafted a plan for a final offensive, and he assigned the most difficult fighting sector – the dense Argonne Forest and the vast Meuse River valley – to

The Allies suffered great losses for more than two years before America declared war. Even after America's entry into World War I, the Allies carried much of the burden. Yet it does not diminish the Allied contributions to say that Americans won the war. The sheer numbers of fresh American soldiers shifted the balance of fighting in favor of the Allies. *National World War I Museum and Memorial, Kansas City, Missouri.*

WILLIE RECEIVES THE MEDAL OF HONOR

the American Expeditionary Forces under General John J. Pershing. In the Argonne forest, Sandlin and the American doughboys faced thick terrain, heavily defended by the German army. From September 26 to the armistice on November 11, American forces suffered more than 20,000 casualties per week, but they eventually earned a fiercely fought victory that played a major role in ending World War I.[3]

Sandlin and the men of the 33rd Division had arrived on France's bloody Western Front in time to take part in the Battle of the Argonne Forest. The Meuse-Argonne Offensive, also known as the Battle of the Argonne Forest, was a major part of the final Allied offensive of World War I that stretched along the entire Western Front. It was fought from September 26, 1918, until the Armistice of November 11, 1918, a total of 47 days. The Meuse-Argonne Offensive was the largest in United States military history, involving 1.2 million American soldiers. It was one of a series of Allied attacks known as the Hundred Days Offensive, which brought the war to an end.

In the summer of 1918, a soldier from the 33rd wrote to his uncle in Lexington, Kentucky, from the trenches "somewhere in France."

> *We first came out from the front line after a two weeks' stay and were met with an order saying we would return in forty-eight hours, so you see we are getting very little rest. The enemy is certainly on the run and if possible we will keep him going, and to do it means hard work for everybody. Everybody seems more than willing to do their part so we might end it all soon. I guess the papers tell you what good work everyone is doing.*
>
> *One cannot realize what things really are over here until they see for themselves. It is terrible, but, of course, it looks bright for us at the present and everybody seems quite happy and is holding up under the hard work. We think here that it*

SERGEANT SANDLIN

can't last longer than one year more, if that long.
I took a patrol out not long ago and got myself a German pistol and a pair of field glasses from an officer. [4]

The battle cost 28,000 German lives and 26,277 American lives, making it the largest and bloodiest operation of World War I for the AEF. [5] American losses were exacerbated by the inexperience of many of the troops and ineffective tactics used during the early phases of the operation. Sandlin and his men were in several battles during the summer of 1918.

> *The Battle of the Argonne Forest, was a major part of the final Allied offensive of World War I that stretched along the entire Western Front.* **The battle cost 28,000 German lives and 26,277 American lives**, *making it the largest and bloodiest operation of World War I for the AEF.*

Then at Bois de Forges, France, on September 26, 1918, Sandlin emerged as one of the greatest heroes of World War I. Sandlin was in charge of a platoon of 59 men when the day began. Following an all-night barrage by 3928 Allied guns, Sandlin's platoon was ordered to advance toward a specific, important military objective. The line had been fighting for hours, advancing slowly, when the Allied forces were stopped by withering fire from carefully placed German machine gun nests, two guns to each nest. At 7:00 am, orders were given to "halt and lie down." While others were trying to stay below the hail of deadly gunfire, Willie Sandlin had a rendezvous with destiny that changed his life forever. Sandlin observed a narrow lane between the firing line of the two guns. Arming himself with four hand grenades, an automatic pistol, and a rifle, he charged the nests alone. Advancing within seventy-five yards of the guns, he threw his first grenade, which fell short and exploded without effect. He raced forward while the enemy emptied two automatic revolvers at him. When he was less than fifty

Willie Sandlin, acting alone, attacked and disabled three German machine gun nests and killed twenty-four German soldiers on September 26, 1918. *National World War I Museum and Memorial, Kansas City, Missouri.*

SERGEANT SANDLIN

yards away from the intense machine gun fire, he threw his second grenade, which struck the nest. He then threw two more grenades, charged the nest, and killed three more German soldiers with his bayonet, making a total of eight enemy combatants that he killed there. Sandlin's platoon advanced and he again took command of his men. The Americans moved forward and flanked another machine gun nest and Sandlin dispatched it in the same way, utilizing grenades. When his grenades were spent, four men still defended the nest. Sandlin had killed them all with his bayonet by the time his platoon arrived. The line continued to advance and at 2:00 pm Sandlin destroyed a third German machine gun nest and its occupants in similar fashion. His heroic assaults resulted in the death of twenty-four German soldiers and the capture of 200 more German soldiers. [6]

> *In Bois de Forges, France, on September 26, 1918, Willie Sandlin destroyed three German machine gun nests and its occupants in similar fashion.* **His heroic assaults resulted in the death of twenty-four German soldiers** *and the capture of 200 more German soldiers.*

"During the day's fighting, Sandlin voluntarily and deliberately ran into the jaws of death, into dangers so great that he could hardly hope to come out with his life." Later that day, Sandlin was slightly wounded by shrapnel in his right hand and forehead. A small piece of shrapnel remained in his forehead and his hand bore scars for a lifetime. Sandlin's commander, General John J. "Black Jack" Pershing, praised him for "conspicuous gallantry and intrepidity above and beyond the call of duty" and recommended him for the Medal of Honor, detailing his heroic actions and praising the twenty-eight-year-old Sandlin's "splendid example of bravery and coolness to his men." Pershing would later describe Sandlin as the outstanding regular army soldier of World War I. [7]

WILLIE RECEIVES THE MEDAL OF HONOR

Gen. John J. Pershing's diary entry for September 26 reads:

> *At 5:30 in the morning we began an attack from the Meuse to the west of the Argonne Forest. In the front line I had three corps of three divisions each: General Bullard with the 3rd Corps on the right, having as his Division Commanders General George Hall with the 33rd, General Cronkhite with the 80th and General Hines with the 4th; General Cameron with the 5th Corps, having General Kuhn with the 79th, General Farnsworth with the 37th and General Johnston with the 91st; and General Liggett with the 1st Corps on the left, having General Alexander with the 77th, General Traub with the 35th and General Blair with the 28th. The attack progressed well during the first part of the day. The 79th was held up in front of Montfaucon about the middle of the day. This ended its advance. The 33rd and 80th Divisions did well. The 4th Division somewhat better than the 33rd and 80th. The 37th, 35th and 28th were less satisfactory. They were raw, their staffs did not work particularly well, and they generally presented the failings of green troops. The most serious problem of the day was mending the roads across what had been No Man's Land. This was a very difficult proposition because all of this ground has been fought over since the beginning of the war and absolutely every trace of the former roads there was lost. The afternoon saw columns of artillery, ammunition and supplies attempting to get over hastily made roads which were narrow and bad, but by night sufficient artillery had crossed and orders were given for the units to organize and resume the attack the next day.* [8]

That same day Sandlin also captured a hospital group and killed the

Willie Sandlin, February 1919, at Chaumont, the general headquarters of the AEF. Sandlin's Medal of Honor was presented to him at Chaumont by General Pershing before Sandlin returned to the United States. *National Archives.*

WILLIE RECEIVES THE MEDAL OF HONOR

commanding officer with his own gun – a Luger which Sandlin wrestled from him in hand-to-hand combat. Sandlin brought that weapon home as a souvenir. Later that day, Sandlin's platoon was involved in the major objective of the day – taking the German battalion headquarters. Many soldiers participated in "this kill" and no individual awards were issued. On October 9, 1918, Sandlin was gassed in the Argonne Forest fighting, but he refused to go to the hospital. Earlier, he suffered a shrapnel wound in his left leg on July 4 at Hamel in the Amiens sector. [9]

More than 300 Kentuckians received special honors in World War I, but Sandlin's feats were a shining example of the "superior courage" shown by American soldiers in battle. The Medal of Honor, sometimes incorrectly called the Congressional Medal of Honor, is awarded by Congress based on a recommendation of the Commanding General. It is the highest honor an American soldier can receive for personal bravery, comparable to Great Britain's Victoria Cross. Ninety American soldiers received the Medal of Honor during World War I — approximately one for every 15,000 men in battle. Nine, including Sandlin's, came from the 132nd Infantry Division.

John J. Pershing cabled the following recommendation:

> *Sergt. Willie Sandlin, Company A. 132nd Infantry (A.S. No. 278103). For conspicuous gallantry and intrepidity above and beyond the call of duty with the enemy at Bois de Forges, France, September 26, 1918. Sergt. Sandlin showed conspicuous gallantry in action at Bois de Forges, on September 26, by advancing alone directly on a machine gun nest which was holding up the line with its fire. He killed the crew with a grenade and enabled the line to advance. Later in the day Sergt. Sandlin attacked alone and put out of action two other machine gun nests, setting a splendid example of bravery and coolness to his men.*

SERGEANT SANDLIN

Finally, in November 1918, the Battle of the Meuse-Argonne Forest had ended. Almost 1,250,000 American troops had participated in defeating the German Army. On November 8, German delegates met with Allied officials to discuss an armistice, and the following day the Kaiser abdicated and fled to the Netherlands. The fighting finally ended on the eleventh hour of the eleventh day of the eleventh month, 1918. After four grim, bloody years of fighting, the war was over.

> ***Willie Sandlin's Medal of Honor was presented to him by General Pershing in February of 1919 at Chaumont, the general headquarters of the AEF.***

Sandlin's Medal of Honor was presented to him by General Pershing in February of 1919 at Chaumont, the general headquarters of the AEF. [10] A month earlier, on January 9, 1919, General Pershing sent a 24-page cablegram to Secretary of War Newton D. Baker, containing "one hundred acts of individual heroism . . ." Supposedly Baker had asked for the stories which would be used in future fundraising efforts. The information was distributed to the press through governmental information agencies. It appeared as a series published in *The Ladies Home Journal* during the summer of 1919 (June, July, and August). One of the individuals identified as one of Pershing's Hundred Heroes was Willie Sandlin, a short account (without a photograph) of his actions appeared on page eighty-nine of the June 1919 edition of *The Ladies Home Journal*.

The next month, on February 1, Pershing's "one hundred best stories of the war" were turned over to the Liberty Loan bureau for publication during the next loan campaign. Some of these stories of heroism were used as newspaper advertisements, some as moving pictures scenarios, and others in pamphlets for public speakers and school children. [11]

Ernest Hemingway would later refer to the Great War as "the most colossal, murderous, mismanaged butchery that has ever taken place on earth." Of the men of all nations in uniform, 8.5 million died. American casualties

WILLIE RECEIVES THE MEDAL OF HONOR

A film of the February 1919 Medal of Honor ceremonies at Chaumont was discovered in the National Archives. This photo is a still from the film. Sandlin is across from Pershing's left shoulder, fourth from the right. *Photo provided by Adam VanKirk.*

totaled 320,710. When the shooting stopped in 1918, the world was no safer and no more democratic that it had been four years earlier, but those were matters for world leaders and diplomats to consider. Sandlin and the millions of men who had fought the war felt an overwhelming, joyous relief. Willie Sandlin had survived and emerged as a hero, and Willie was on his way home.

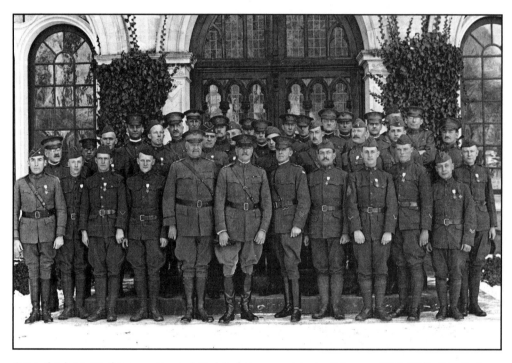

General John J. Pershing, center, and Medal of Honor recipients, February 1919. Willie Sandlin is on the front row, third from the left. *National Archives.*

Members of the 132nd Infantry Regiment 33rd Division in front line trench expecting an attack. From the trench can be seen the Valley of the Meuse, where an estimated 70,000 men are buried. *Library of Congress.*

Members of the 33rd Division take advantage of the camouflage left by German troops during the American Meuse-Argonne Offensive. *U. S. Army Signal Corps photograph, October 3, 1918.*

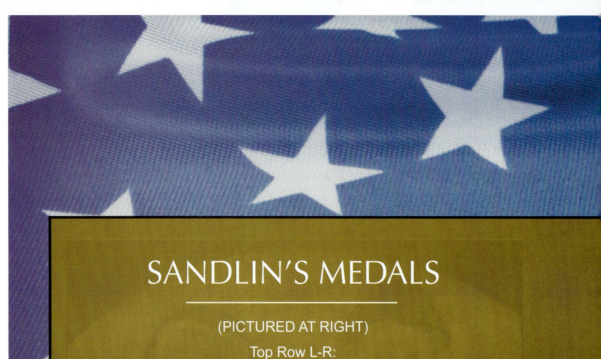

SANDLIN'S MEDALS

(PICTURED AT RIGHT)

Top Row L-R:

United States – Medal of Honor
France – Medaille Militaire (Military Medal)
France – Croix de Guerre w/Palm
Italy – Croce al Merito di Guerra (War Merit Cross)

Second Row:
U. S. Army Marksmanship Badge – Expert Rifleman

Third Row L-R:
Unknown Badge/Pin
Veterans of Foreign Wars (VFW) Medal

MEDAL OF HONOR

90 Medals of Honor were awarded for acts in the World War. Nine MOHs were awarded to members of Sandlin's 33rd Infantry Division. Sandlin was awarded his medal of honor on February 9, 1919.

The Sandlin artifacts are an important part of the Kentucky Historical Society collection.

PURPLE HEART

The Purple Heart was created in 1933, years after Sandlin's war efforts. However, it was originally not a war wound medal but a medal for Merit. Any World War I soldier who had a Certificate of Merit signed by Pershing could turn it in and receive the medal. This is how Willie earned his Purple Heart.

LEGION OF MERIT

Sandlin appears to have also somehow received the Legion of Merit, established in 1942. The medal could not have been his son's, as he did not see active service, so it must have been gifted to him by someone who simply thought he deserved it.

BRONZE STAR

Sandlin also has a Bronze Star, established in 1944. The medal must have also been gifted to Willie.

U.S ARMY MARKSMANSHIP BADGE

This Expert Rifleman Badge was given for extraordinary skill with a rifle. Willie received this medal on June 12, 1916.

WORLD WAR I VICTORY MEDAL

Every soldier who was in the service during World War I received this victory medal.

FOREIGN DECORATIONS

WAR CROSS

FRANCE – The Croix de Guerre 1914–1918 (War Cross) is a French military decoration, created to recognize French and allied soldiers who were cited for valorous service during World War I. Sandlin received his medal with Bronze palm (palme de bronze), which was for those who were cited at the army level. It was given to him along with the Médaille militaire, his other French decoration, when he was still in France on May 7, 1919.

MILITARY MEDAL

FRANCE – The Médaille Militaire (Military Medal) is one of the foremost French military decorations. Sandlin received this medal in France on May 7, 1919.

WAR MERIT CROSS

ITALY – Croce al Merito di Guerra (War Merit Cross) An Italian decoration established for World War I, the War Merit Cross was awarded to members of the armed forces after a minimum of one year of service in the trenches or elsewhere, in contact with an enemy. Sandlin did not receive this medal until 1921.

MEDAL FOR MILITARY BRAVERY

MONTENEGRO – Medaille pour la Bravoure Militaire (Medal for military bravery). Maybe it fell out of his pocket or perhaps he let his children play with it too much, but Sandlin seems to have lost this medal. He requested another from the Yugoslavian government, but was denied it as they did not have record of the award.

OTHER MEDALS

VFW MEMBERSHIP MEDAL

This medal was given to members of the Veterans of Foreign Wars, an organization prominent in Sandlin's life.

The family collection of Sandlin's medals. For more information on the medals that Willie received, see Appendix A.

Left: The *Mount Vernon* in New York Harbor, July 8, 1918. Willie Sandlin returned to America on the *Mount Vernon*.

Below: Troops on board the *USS Mount Vernon*, 1919.

Photos courtesy of John Trowbridge.

WILLIE RECEIVES THE MEDAL OF HONOR

Home and Back to Europe Again

After his heroics in France, Sandlin returned to the United States. Newspapers later proclaimed that he had been "one of the conspicuous heroes of the great war, yet his remarkable feat . . . has not been given to the public." For example, on February 5, 1919, *The Lexington Leader* mentioned Sandlin's feats in three lines on page 8, a total of sixteen words. Sandlin was later offered an "attractive position" as an army recruiting sergeant but said he "had enough of army life." [12] Upon his arrival in New York, he met Florence Norwood, a woman who befriended the young soldier and took an interest in his life. She later sent gifts to the Sandlin children after Willie and Belvia married. She was so well-liked that Willie and Belvia named their youngest daughter after her. "She came to visit us once when I was about six years old," remembered Florence. Willie was discharged from the Army on May 30, 1919, at Camp Grant in Rockford, Illinois. [13] Two months later, on July 22, 1919, *The Lexington Leader* carried a front page article on Sandlin's Medal of Honor heroics.

Almost two million doughboys returned from the Great War in 1919. Many were disillusioned. Some had seen the hell of modern warfare, and they had lost their enthusiasm for parades and displays of patriotism. Others had experienced the boredom and mindless regimentation of training camps. Not Willie. He was thrilled to be home! He returned to Leslie County for half a year. At that time, there were no highways or railroads in Leslie County, so Willie rode the L & N Railroad to the Altro Station near Hazard and then walked home by a route that included Long's Creek. On his first night home from the war, Willie stayed with relatives at Long's Creek and told them about his war experiences. He had been told that his medals "would bring him much notice and publicity," so the bashful and modest young man "who had dared every danger of the enemy . . . shrank from publicity and hid his medals, the telltale of his wonderful deeds." After he returned to Hyden, he said that he had had "only two really happy days in my life. One was the day General Pershing pinned the Medal of Honor on my breast and the other was the day I returned home." [14]

According to W. H. Lewis, the County Historian for Leslie County during World War I, other Leslie County men who were wounded in World War I included the following:

Wilson Young, Warbranch	Allen Howard, Asher
Allen Howard, Wooton	Robert Emory Johnson, Shoal
Theodore Adams, Cutshin	James Morgan, Hoskinston
Sam Joseph, Daley	Jasper Roberts, Roark
Wm. Jesse Anderson, Warbranch	Berg Wooton, Wooton
Oscar Morgan, Hoskinston	Wm. O. Bradley, Obed
Dan Asher, Hyden	Wayne Bowling, Hyden
Salmon Taylor, Helton	Adam Brock, Warbranch
Curt Begley, Dry Hill	Heywood Caldwood, Obed
Irvin Wooton, Wooton	Monroe Estridge, Confluence
Bradley Bowling, Shoal	Irving Eversole, Wooton
Carr Helton, Warbranch	Pearl B. Gay, Shoal
Horace E. Gay, Shoal	James Hoskins, Asher

The following men from Leslie County were killed in action:

Arthur Dale Bond, Hyden	Wm. N. Hoskins, Hoskinston
George Pennington, Warbranch	Bertel Roberts, Hyden
George Roark, Roark	Noah Sizemore, Roark
John Valentine, Confluence	Oscar Morgan, Hoskinston

WILLIE RECEIVES THE MEDAL OF HONOR

His Brother's Keeper

Although Willie Sandlin never led an easy life as a soldier or a civilian, he did not use personal problems as an excuse when a family member needed help. Shortly after the war, the five Sandlin brothers – all veterans of World War I – returned to Leslie County. Willie, Charlie, and John remained in Leslie County; Sonny returned to Breathitt County, and Mathy married a girl from Maryland and settled there. Willie's brother Charlie had been honorably discharged from the Army in 1918 because of physical disabilities. In February 1919, he was convicted of manslaughter in the death of Arthur Jones and sentenced to a two-year term in prison. After six months, he was pardoned by Governor Black because county officials, eleven of the jurors, and relatives of the victim petitioned for a pardon. After weighing evidence and information from the victim's father, mother, brothers, and sisters, the Governor declared the killing was accidental and issued a pardon on November 12, 1919. The following day, he explained he had been "besieged by pardon applications since the election." He refused most of the applications, but granted a few where clemency was merited and a pardon was "best for the prisoner and society." Sergeant Willie Sandlin took the pardon to his brother.

Twelve years later, Charlie was in jail in Hazard after the fatal shooting of thirty-eight-year-old James Jones. Jones was killed during an attempted armed robbery. James had gone to Charlie Sandlin's home and asked him to open his store because he was hungry. The store was at Homersville, ten miles from Hyden on Hell for Certain Creek. Just as Sandlin opened the door, Jones drew a gun on Sandlin who then drew his own gun and shot Jones five times. Funeral services were held for Jones two days after he died. [15] Charlie survived these conflicts and became a deputy sheriff in Leslie County. He died at home of a heart attack on October 19, 1950, when he was 61 years old.

On December 9, 1919, Sandlin was in Lexington to assist with the parade

DESCRIPTION OF APPLICANT.

Age: 29 years.
Stature: 5 feet, 7 inches, Eng.
Forehead: High
Eyes: Brown
Nose: straight
Mouth: medium
Chin: round
Hair: brown
Complexion: fair
Face: oval
Distinguishing marks: _____

IDENTIFICATION.

_____, 19___

I, _____, solemnly swear that I am a { native / naturalized } citizen of the United States; that I resided at _____; that I have known the above-named _____ personally for ___ years and know { him / her } to be a native citizen of the United States; and that the facts stated in { his / her } affidavit are true to the best of my knowledge and belief.

_____
(Occupation.)

_____
(Address of witness.)

Sworn to before me this ___ day of _____, 19___

[SEAL.]

_____
Clerk of the _____ Court at _____

Applicant desires passport to be sent to the following address:

Capt. O. L. Smith
City Hall

A signed duplicate of the photograph to be attached hereto must be sent to the Department with the application.

Willie Sandlin's passport application, December 18, 1919.

Personally appeared before me, a Notary Public, one C. B. Donnelly , who after being properly identified, on oath says:

That Sgt. Willie Sandlin is an applicant for American passport and that he has known Sgt. Sandlin and his people for the past five or six years and know that they are residents of the State of Kentucky. That from the records of said Sandlin filed in the office of the Hon. J. M. Robsion, M. C., for whom the affiant is Secretary, the said Sandlin was born in Breathitt County, Ky., on Jan. 1st 1890.

C. B. Donnelly
Signature of Affiant.

Subscribed and sworn to before me this 27th day of Dec. 1919.

Wayne W. Cordell
Notary Public

Seal

(Disposition of passport.)

OATH OF ALLEGIANCE.

Further, I do solemnly swear that I will support and defend the Constitution of the United States against all enemies, foreign and domestic; that I will bear true faith and allegiance to the same; and that I take this obligation freely, without any mental reservation or purpose of evasion: So help me God.

Mabel O'Callaghan
(Signature of applicant.)

Sworn to before me this DEC 18 1919 day of _____, 19__

[SEAL OF PASSPORT AGENCY.]

Passport Agent, Department of State.

FEE REC'D. DEC 27

12910

* A person born in the United States should submit a birth certificate with his application, or if the birth was not officially recorded, affidavits from the attending physician, parents, or other persons having actual knowledge of the birth.

[OVER.]

Willie Sandlin's passport application, December 18, 1919.

SERGEANT SANDLIN

that attended the inauguration of Governor Edwin P. Morrow. [16] Later that month, because of his exemplary military record, Willie was appointed special escort for the bodies of soldiers who had died overseas. Sandlin left for France in January 1920, accompanied by Miss Jessie Dell, who took charge of the office that responded to families of American soldiers buried in Europe. Sandlin was an example of the "splendid men" the War Department sent to France to handle the return "of the bodies of our soldiers," reported a newspaper in Kansas. "It is only fitting that men who have made such splendid records in the war should now . . . bring home the bodies of their comrades . . . ." In response to this important assignment, Sandlin said that it was a "great honor" to assist in the work "which means so much to so many thousands of American homes." His appointment came from Secretary of War Newton D. Baker on the recommendation of Major General Harry L. Rogers, Quartermaster General of the American Expeditionary Force in France. In 1920, Sandlin worked as a graves checker for the Graves Registration Bureau, checking graves in Belgium, France, Luxembourg, Italy, and England. [17] In May 1920, Sandlin declared that he was "opposed to the plan" of returning the bodies of American soldiers to their homes in the United States. Based on his experience in France after the war, Sandlin called the plan "impractical" and said "those who made the supreme sacrifice should lie where they died." Sandlin cited another reason for his opposition to returning the bodies of those who made the supreme sacrifice for their country. "In many instances," said Sandlin, "the effects of gun fire, gas

> *In May 1920,* **Sandlin declared that he was "opposed to the plan" of returning the bodies of American soldiers to their homes in the United States.** *Based on his experience in France after the war, Sandlin called the plan "impractical" and said "those who made the supreme sacrifice should lie where they died."*

and bombing left no means by which large numbers of men could properly be identified." [18]

Sandlin had been in Lexington with a friend when he was interviewed about his feelings about returning America's dead from Europe. "An attempt was made to have him attend the unveiling of the memorial tablet to Kentucky soldiers at the University of Kentucky," but the "big sergeant" refused "the invitation, fearing that he would be called upon to speak." [19]

In this cherished family photograph, Belvia is 47 years old, and this photo shows her as a healthy and attractive wife and mother. *Florence Muncy Collection.*
Willie's daughter Leona remembers her father as a hard worker who "liked to farm."
On November 26, 1927, Willie and Belvia purchased farm land on Ellis Creek. On May 22, 1937, Belvia's father William Roberts deeded land on Owls Creek to Willie and Belvia.
Information courtesy of Mary Wooton.

Where there's life, there's hope.
Tarzan
Edgar Rice Burroughs

CHAPTER FOUR
MARRIAGE, EARLY FAMILY LIFE, AND THE COMMUNITY

Sandlin then returned home to eastern Kentucky. On June 4, 1920, he married Belvia Roberts, a woman he began courting at a box dinner social after he first returned from Europe. They were married in the Presbyterian Church in Hyden. Their happy marriage produced one son and four daughters who reached adulthood; Vorres, born in 1921, followed by Leona, Nancy Ruth, Florence, and Robert E. Lee Sandlin. Cora and Rose died of childhood diseases before their fourth birthdays.

Willie is holding Cora. Belvia is holding the baby, Leona, and Vorres is standing next to her mother. For more information on Willie's family, see the chart on page 88. *Florence Muncy Collection.*

WILLIE AND BELVIA'S FAMILY

Willie Sandlin (January 1, 1890 - May 29, 1949)
Belvia Roberts Sandlin (June 16, 1902 - February 5, 1999)
Married June 4, 1920

Children:
- Vorres Sandlin Day (April 19, 1921 - December 25, 2015)
- Cora Wilson Stewart Sandlin (December 15, 1922 - October 2, 1925)
- Leona Sandlin Nichols (February 11, 1925 - Living)
- Nancy Ruth Sandlin Brewer (December 28, 1926 - September 19, 1998)
- Florence Norwood Sandlin Muncy (January 31, 1929 - Living)
- Robert E. Lee Sandlin (November 2, 1932 - June 22, 2005)
- Rose Sandlin (May 9, 1933 - November 11, 1936)

On the names of the Sandlin children:
- Vorres Sandlin was named for Jon Vorres who befriended Willie while he was in France.
- Cora Wilson Stewart Sandlin was named after the famous literacy advocate, founder of the Moonlight Schools, and intimate friend of the Sandlin family.
- Leona Sandlin was named after Leona Morgan, the midwife who helped to deliver her.
- Nancy Ruth Sandlin was named after Ruth Houston, a wealthy Pennsylvanian who did humanitarian work in Appalachia. This woman's parents owned a steel company.
- Florence Norwood Sandlin was named after a woman who met Willie in New York when he returned from the war. She later visited the Sandlin family in Hyden.
- Robert E. Lee Sandlin was named for Robert E. Lee Murphy, the man who led the failed Veterans of Foreign Wars campaign to raise funds to purchase land and a home for the Sandlin family. In a place and time dominated by Republicans, naming a child Robert E. Lee was also Willie's way of affirming that he was a proud Democrat. When Willie ran for political office, he ran as an independent, because he refused to run as a Republican and was ensured a loss as a Democrat.

MARRIAGE, EARLY FAMILY LIFE, AND THE COMMUNITY

Willie and Belvia began their married life on a rental farm in Breathitt County and later moved their family to the "weaning house" on the Roberts property. The "weaning house" was a small house the Roberts built near their home so that when their children married, they would have a starter home to wean them of parental support. The Sandlins arrived at the Roberts home with a mule and a few personal possessions, including a trunk that contained some interesting souvenirs of WWI. Sandlin did not mind showing a Luger pistol that he took from a German officer, but he was extremely shy about showing the medals which were stuffed in his pockets when he returned to the Leslie County hills in 1919. With some coaxing, Mrs. Sandlin would show Willie's medals to visitors. They included the Medal of Honor, the Croix de Guerre (with palm), the Medal Militaires of France, the Italian War Cross, and the Montenegrin War Cross.[1]

Rose, the Sandlin's youngest child, died of meningitis when she was three and a half years old. She is buried with her sister Cora in the William Roberts cemetery. *Sandlin Family Collection.*

When their first child was a baby, Willie, "the champion Hun Killer of Kentucky" according to the local press, took a job as a security guard at the "Old Joe Distillery" in Anderson County. He had been appointed to the revenue force "in the spring of 1922 and was on duty at the J.B. Ripy plant in Tyrone before he worked at Old Joe's Distillery." The *Louisville Courier-Journal* praised Sandlin's appointment and observed that if "seekers for public office were chosen as discriminatingly to fit the job, how government would improve." In sharp contrast, a lengthy article in the same newspaper ridiculed distillery guard as a "sitting down job" and argued that "each position of distillery guard is indicative of the disposition of mankind to seek the soft snap . . . ." In truth, it was a hard and dangerous job and newspapers in Kentucky regularly reported armed-robbery attempts and resulting gun battles at central Kentucky distilleries. For example, on November 18, 1921, guards at the W. B Suffell distillery, near Lawrenceburg, "fought a gun battle with three men who apparently were trying to rob the distillery warehouse." [2] By December, 1922, forty-nine federal distillery guards, including Willie Sandlin, had been laid off "because of the shortage of prohibition funds." However, an article entitled "Too Tame For Warrior" in *The Lexington Leader* reported that Sandlin "had resigned his position as guard at the Old Joe Distillery" after having "been on duty at various Anderson County plants for several months. [3] He may have been laid off or he may have resigned, but Willie and his family returned to Leslie County.

> *During the 1920s, after Willie had returned home and married,* **America experienced a period of material growth and societal changes known as the "Roaring Twenties."** *It was a time of quick wealth, youthful disillusionments, and changing social and moral values.*

The Sandlins soon moved back to the "weaning house" and Willie's father-in-law loaned Willie the money to purchase a small farm with a house on the property. Florence was born at that house with the assistance of a nurse from the Frontier Nursing Service. [4]

During the 1920s, after Willie had returned home and married, America experienced a period of material growth and societal changes known as the "Roaring Twenties." It was a time of quick wealth, youthful disillusionments, and changing social and moral values. In the first two decades of the twentieth century, America grew in population and became more industrialized. In the mainstream world, paved roads, telephones, electricity, and the automobile brought Sandlin's generation into a more mechanized world that allowed

After World War I, automobiles were everywhere, eventually prompting rural counties, like Leslie County, to improve their road systems. In the early 1920s, for just $290 ($5 a week on the installment plan) rural Americans could purchase a Model T runabout. *Detroit Public Library's Automotive History Division.*

SERGEANT SANDLIN

Americans more time for entertainment. Between 1920 and 1930, the number of passenger cars registered in the United States rose from 8 million to 23 million, an average of one car for every six citizens. However, many of these societal changes had not filtered down to Leslie County in the 1920s, and Willie Sandlin and his neighbors lived more conservative and more economically challenged lives than their mainstream contemporaries.

The decade of the 1920s, the decade when Sandlin married and started a family, was, according to the great historian Bruce Catton, "the gaudiest, the saddest, and the most misinterpreted era in modern American history." It was a time of prohibition, bootleggers, the Charleston, Washington scandals, Chicago gangsters, and the symbol of the age, the Flapper. As Catton observes, that was, at best, "only a partial picture." Willie and Belvia Sandlin represented millions of Americans in the 1920s who were "serious, hard-working people who did their best to earn a living, bring up their children, live decently . . . and put away a few dollars for old age." [5]

Recognition for a War Hero

Willie Sandlin never presented himself as a celebrity. He was too modest to seek public adoration and too shy to enjoy the attention of the media. For example, in 1922 *The Lexington Leader* brought news of another eastern Kentucky war hero, Sergeant Samuel Joseph, who was badly wounded in the Battle of the Argonne Forest. Joseph had served on the front lines "without getting a scratch." Then in the Argonne fighting, "he was hit 102 times" and "had sixty-two bullets taken from his body." Joseph was hospitalized for 28 months and endured several operations before returning home to resume civilian life as a student at Sue Bennett Memorial School in London, Kentucky. Although the newspaper argued that "sergeants won the war" it made no mention of Willie Sandlin, while comparing Joseph to Sergeant York and Sergeant Woodfill.

The Leslie County newspaper, *Thousandsticks*, picked up this story, and

MARRIAGE, EARLY FAMILY LIFE, AND THE COMMUNITY

clarified Joseph's background: he was born and raised in Leslie County on the head of Polls Creek, near Daley, and lived there until "he was called to the colors." Like the Lexington newspaper, Sandlin's hometown paper made no mention of him. Instead they compared Joseph to Abraham Lincoln and observed that both men "were raised in the country and on a farm." [6]

Sandlin, on several occasions, attended local and national meetings where he was recognized as a Medal of Honor recipient. For example, in September 1919, Sandlin and 131-year-old "Uncle John" Shell, "the oldest man in the world," met with the Lexington Board of Commerce in the ballroom of the Phoenix Hotel. However, Sandlin "declined" an opportunity to discuss his war experiences. According to *The Lexington Herald*, Laurel Countians "believed so much in Sandlin that they raised a purse of $300, presented to him to spend as he pleases in having a good time." His friends and neighbors proudly opined that Willie had "a record more glorious that Alvin York's. He's out of Alvin York's class," observed R. B. Roberts, Commonwealth Attorney for the 33rd judicial district. [7]

> *In 1921,* **Sandlin was among 25 Medal of Honor recipients who attended the "greatest gathering in the history of American heroes"** *at the annual convention of the American Legion at Kansas City, Missouri.*

In 1921, Sandlin was among 25 Medal of Honor recipients who attended the "greatest gathering in the history of American heroes" at the annual convention of the American Legion at Kansas City, Missouri. The following year, the members of the American Legion gathered in New Orleans for their annual convention. The Legion invited all Medal of Honor recipients with the promise that their travel and housing expenses would be paid. Sandlin was among more than twenty heroes who accepted the invitation. Later, in a Fourth of July speech in Lexington in 1924, he said, "I am glad to be here. I thank you for your

SERGEANT SANDLIN

Sandlin often attended VFW meetings, particularly in Lexington, Kentucky, and this one in Frankfort. Bottom row, left to right: Colonel J. W. Stover, millionaire coal operator from Georgia; Honorable J. W. Fields, Governor of Kentucky; Honorable Denhart, Lieutenant Governor of Kentucky. Top row, left to right: Mr. DeGot, commander VFW post, Louisville; commander, VFW post, Ashland; Colonel Gaines, head of the American Flag Campaign, Frankfort; Sergeant Samuel Woodfill, Medal of Honor recipient from Indiana; R. E. L. Murphy, National officer VFW, Lexington; Sergeant Sandlin; Mr. Votaw, commander VFW post, Lexington; brother to the commander of the Ashland VFW post. *Photo courtesy of the Western Kentucky University Library and Archives.*

hospitality. When I was in the fields of France, my heart was in the hills of Kentucky. I will now step aside and let you hear the real speakers." According to a December 11, 1924, article in the *Tyrone (PA) Daily Herald*, "Sandlin's speech was the shortest and the applause was the longest on the day's program of orations." After the day's events, he refused invitations to stay on as a guest because he was eager to "get back to the hills." That same year, Sandlin was "the honored guest" at a VFW meeting in Lexington, where he was given a 20-year membership. In the 1920s, state newspapers reported that Sandlin had "declined to permit his life story to be written for motion picture use."

Throughout the 1920s and 1930s, the Lexington newspapers regularly reported Sandlin's involvement with the VFW chapter in Lexington. On

MARRIAGE, EARLY FAMILY LIFE, AND THE COMMUNITY

September 6, 1924, Sandlin was a member of the Kentucky delegation to the twenty-fifth encampment of the Veterans of Foreign Wars, which met in Atlantic City. Prior to their encampment, "four of America's greatest heroes called on President Coolidge at the White House. Sergeant Samuel Woodfill headed the delegation, which included Sergeant Willie Sandlin, Lieutenant Jesse O. Creech, and Robert E. Lee Murphy." The conclusion of the twenty-fifth (Silver Jubilee) Encampment of the VFW included a "Defense Test" parade of approximately 25,000 veterans. The parade was held in Atlantic City on September 12, 1924, and billed as "the last official act of General John J. Pershing as Commander-in-Chief of the Armies of the United States." Pershing was the reviewing officer of a marching body of men who had fought with him in American battles for four decades. Among the ranks were "four veterans of the Mexican War of 1846."

Included on the reviewing stand was General Lloyd M. Brett, Commander-in-Chief of the VFW. Brett had been at West Point seven years before Pershing and "the grizzled commander" had been in the active service of the regular army for more than forty years. Samuel Woodfill and Willie Sandlin, two members of the Kentucky delegation who wore the Medal of Honor, served as Pershing's aides. [8]

In 1925, Medal of Honor recipient Willie Sandlin, a member of the Hugh McKee Post of the Lexington, was a prominent member of Kentucky's delegation to the VFW's national encampment in Tulsa, Oklahoma from August 30 to September 4. In addition to Sandlin, the Lexington delegation included Captain Robert E. Lee Murphy, commander of the department of Kentucky; Reverend J. B. Head from Versailles who presided as national chaplain of the encampment; Oliver K. Barlow, commander of the Hugh McKee post who wore "two medals and three wound stripes for injuries suffered in France;" J. B. Eversole, a veteran of the Spanish-American War; and John F. Quinn. The group departed from Louisville in a special railroad car on the night of August 28.

Sandlin's relationship with Robert E. Lee Murphy was a mixed blessing, at best. Murphy's introduction of Sandlin at the Tulsa meeting was unprofessional

Sergeant Willie Sandlin, President Calvin Coolidge, and Sergeant Sam Woodfill, September 5, 1924.

Left: After World War I ended, John Joseph "Black Jack" Pershing was promoted to General of the Armies of the United States. There was a movement to draft Pershing as a candidate for President in 1920, but he refused to campaign. He died on July 5, 1948, and was buried in Arlington National Cemetery, near the gravesites of soldiers he commanded in Europe. *Library of Congress.*

MARRIAGE, EARLY FAMILY LIFE, AND THE COMMUNITY

and disrespectful. Perhaps Murphy was trying to develop a colorful reputation for Sandlin or perhaps he had too much to drink, but he said:

> *Anyway, comrades and ladies, we have one more with us who hails from the intersection of Devils Creek and Hells Corner down around Lee County and Breathitt County, Ky. – where they did not have to draft a single man. There is only one post there and that is the Veterans of Foreign War Post. No other organization has been able to meet for five years there. This comrade whom I have reference to enlisted in 1913 and waited until 1918 to perform. On September 26, 1918, in France, this comrade was with his men going forward and held up a machine-gun nest and went in there single-handed, killed eight, and captured two machine guns; they shot him two or three times and gassed him, but it had no effect on him. Twice during that day he did the same thing, accomplished the same feat. He holds the record of killing more men single-handed than any other man in the American Army. He lives in a place where there are no automobiles and no railroad trains to break the peaceful slumber of the inhabitants, but they know it long before we know it when a war is coming. This sergeant has a wife and three beautiful little girl babies and lives back up in these mountains.*
>
> *Oklahoma is settled entirely by Kentuckians; you would not have had a State if it had not been for Kentuckians. That is why it is so great and why I was in favor of coming here.*
>
> *Back up in these mountains that I speak of, where you can not hear anything, they raise coon dogs and have their mountain dew, and they do not allow prohibition officers in that section of the country. Sergeant Woodfill never drank any in*

SERGEANT SANDLIN

> *his life, but Willie Sandlin was never without it, and I take great pleasure in introducing to you Sergt. Willie Sandlin, from Hells Corner and Devils Creek.*

Murphy's ridiculously inaccurate and insulting introduction inspired a direct response from the normally soft-spoken and bashful Medal of Honor recipient. Sandlin rose and said:

> *Comrade Commander in Chief, ladies of the auxiliary, comrades, ladies, and gentlemen, I have only a minute or so, and after all that Comrade Murphy has been telling you about me drinking up all the mountain dew in the hills of Kentucky you may not care to hear me say anything. I do, however, want to say that Comrade Murphy don't know anything about my wife and three babies; he don't know what he is talking about; he never saw my wife. I know, as a V.F.W., that you do not want to hear talk for a minute. I am hungry and I want to get something to eat, and if Oklahoma has any mountain dew, I don't know whether it is varnish or what it is, but possibly if I had some mountain dew I could make a speech. I will say I am glad to be in Tulsa. We have talked about Tulsa, we veterans have, for one year; we wanted to get down here and see the mountain dew. You know we Kentucky people claim we have the proudest people in the world, but we know, of course, Tulsa is next to us. In conclusion, I desire to say that we thank you for the splendid welcome you have given us and to assure you that we deeply appreciate it. I thank you. [Applause.]*

Early in 1926, Sandlin, and fellow Medal of Honor recipient Samuel Woodfill from Fort Thomas, Kentucky, were among the speakers at a banquet

MARRIAGE, EARLY FAMILY LIFE, AND THE COMMUNITY

given by the Kentucky VFW Lodge in Lexington to honor Colonel Fred B. Stover, a Pennsylvanian who served as the VFW's Commander-in-Chief. [9]

For the remainder of the 1920s, Willie Sandlin continued to attend VFW meetings in the hope that the VFW could assist his efforts to receive additional benefits as a wounded, injured, and disabled veteran. The VFW held its state meeting in Lexington in 1927, the same year that Charles Lindbergh made his historic transatlantic flight. Among the many resolutions adopted by almost 2000 veterans of the Great War was one "deploring treatment afforded Sergeant Willie Sandlin by the Veterans Bureau." The following year, Sandlin attended the national meeting of the VFW in Denver.

While Willie was attending the VFW meeting in Denver, on May 26, 1928, his brother Elihu Sandlin, age 35, was shot and killed by twenty-five-year-old Ance Baker on Upper Buffalo Creek in Owsley County. The following month Baker was tried by a jury in the Owsley County Circuit Court.

Judge S. H. Rich of Irvine defended Baker, who claimed self-defense in the killing. Commonwealth Attorney John W. Walker of Beattyville and County Attorney J. K. Gabbard, assisted by Rose & Stamper, Beattyville attorneys, conducted the prosecution. Judge Sam Hunt of Beattyville presided.

The trial began on June 25, 1928, and the verdict was brought in at 11:00 am the following morning. Baker was convicted of manslaughter and sentenced to four years in the State Reformatory. Judge Rich, Baker's attorney, said that Baker would not appeal the verdict. Willie's brother Charlie was present to represent the Sandlin family at the trial. Like his famous brother Willie, Elihu was a World War I veteran. [10]

In 1929, the annual VFW meeting was held in Louisville, with an estimated 50,000 veterans in attendance. Willie was one of the attendees, along with Alvin York and Samuel Woodfill. Each year, when the VFW denounced the Veterans Bureau for not giving benefits to Willie Sandlin, the Veterans Bureau became more defensive, and Sandlin's chances for additional benefits seemed to diminish. [11]

SERGEANT SANDLIN

Of Sandlin's Tennessee counterpart, Alvin York, superior officers often said that "he always seemed instinctively to know the right thing to do." In instinct and values, Sandlin was much like York. He had no personal advisors, but he had a clear set of values and excellent judgment. He refused to accept money or fame for doing his job and meeting his obligations as a soldier. Sandlin was not an avid reader, so he had probably never read a biography of Robert E. Lee, but he had heard stories about Lee from the old men in his community. Unlike other Confederate officers who had "sacrificed their reputations upon the altar of expediency," Lee chose not to profit from his hero status. Perhaps Lee became a role model for Sandlin. That may have been part of the reason Willie named his only son Robert E. Lee Sandlin. Men like Lee, York, and Sandlin had an uncompromising set of values, and they adhered to a strict code of honor. [12]

Alvin York saw his accomplishments as a constant reminder of the power of his faith. *Library of Congress.*

Willie's People

Willie and Belvia lived in a close-knit Appalachian community of people who were loving friends and neighbors. The men "swapped work" in the fields, and the women, who were part of an informal sorority of hard work and high standards, swapped work, too. Before the advent of the Frontier Nursing Service, they were especially helpful to one another during childbirth. When a woman was about to have a baby, she alerted a relative or neighbor who specialized in midwifery. The midwife usually did not do housework. Her

MARRIAGE, EARLY FAMILY LIFE, AND THE COMMUNITY

primary job was to aid the delivery of a healthy baby. If there were no complications, she stayed a few days, but if the new mother was weak or ill, the midwife might stay for several weeks. Sometimes, all she received for her efforts were heartfelt thanks, but more often she was gratefully paid with surplus farm products or return-the-favor services when her own "lying-in" time came.

Willie and Belvia taught their children to swap work. For example, when Sandlin's daughter Florence was in high school, she was part of a two-person cheerleader squad. She traveled to out-of-town basketball games with William Campbell and his wife and their children. To pay the Campbells for transportation, Florence worked for them for free. Every morning on her way to school, Florence stopped and got the Campbell children ready for school, because the parents ran the drugstore and they went to work early. Florence fixed cereal and orange juice for breakfast, and then she braided the little girl's hair before she walked the children to school. On Saturday, Florence was the "soda jerk" at the Campbell's drug store. [13]

Loyal Jones' wonderful book, *Appalachian Values*, captures the people of Hyden and Leslie County who were the Sandlin's friends and neighbors. They were, according to John Stephenson, "determined individuals, families, and communities attempting to construct decent lives." The eleven values, defined by Jones, allow us to see Sandlin's people "from close and afar." They are religion, independence, neighborliness, familism, personalism, humility, love of place, patriotism, sense of beauty, and sense of humor. All of these values are evident in Willie Sandlin's life and culture. In the Appalachian culture that produced Willie Sandlin and millions like him, people love their families, homes, and communities. They believe in the rule of law, and they advocate a concept of justice that is simple, direct, and often inflexible: for every good deed, there is a reward, and for every bad deed, there is a punishment.

In 1925, Mary Carson Breckinridge founded the Frontier Nursing Service an organization she led until her death on May 16, 1965, at Wendover, Leslie County. *Photographic Archives, University of Louisville.*

Being of these hills I cannot pass beyond.
"Heritage"
James Still

CHAPTER FIVE
IMPROVING HIS EASTERN KENTUCKY HOMELAND

Like his more famous counterpart, Tennessee's Alvin York, Sandlin wanted to use his fame and influence to serve his home area. In the years following WWI, eastern Kentuckians were working to improve the quality of life in their mountain homeland. Two of the region's greatest leaders were Cora Wilson Stewart and Mary Breckinridge.

In 1925, Mary Carson Breckinridge founded the Frontier Nursing Service at Hyden, in Leslie County. That year, Breckinridge rode horseback through Leslie County seeking a place to locate the service. When she came to the beautiful, rugged countryside which she named Wendover, she knew she had found the place for her headquarters. The first buildings were erected there in 1925 and dedicated in December of that year. [1]

Breckinridge was from a privileged background. Her grandfather had been vice-president of the United States, and her father had served as United States minister to Russia. Mary attended finishing schools in Switzerland and Connecticut and then earned a nursing degree from St. Luke's Hospital in New

SERGEANT SANDLIN

York City. She later did specialized graduate work in midwifery in both London and New York and became a certified nurse-midwife. Her strong commitment to advancing health care for the poor brought her to Leslie County. Soon Mrs. Breckinridge's nurses, riding on horseback, were providing maternal care and child welfare to more than 10,000 people in an isolated, seven-hundred-square mile section of eastern Kentucky. Two of her strongest supporters were Sergeant Willie Sandlin and his wife Belvia. In her famous autobiography, *Wide Neighborhoods*, Breckinridge reported that Sandlin had "ignored the offers of wealth that could have been his had he gone out to the platform and the radio" and had returned to a modest farm not far from Hyden. He and Belvia "threw themselves into the activities of the Frontier Nursing Service from its beginning" and regularly attended the organization's meetings and shared in its work. [2]

By the early 1930s, the Frontier Nursing Service (FNS) serviced approximately 1,000 square miles through nursing centers scattered over the area. Uniformed nurses and midwives traveled by horseback through rugged mountain country "to attend women in childbirth, to nurse the sick," and to promote the tenets of public health and hygiene. By 1933, the FNS, working cooperatively with federal and state agencies and various health foundations, had given more than 81,000 inoculations against smallpox, diphtheria, typhoid fever, and influenza.

The nursing centers were houses with living accommodations for the nurses and a clinic for the patients. Each nurse covered an area of about 48 square miles and was equipped with two sets of saddlebags – one for general nursing and one for obstetrical care. As a result of their work, the region's infant mortality rate declined considerably and, through their heroic services, not one mother died in childbirth. Before the advent of FNS, untrained "granny women" assisted with childbirth in Leslie County because there was no medical doctor available to serve a population of 10,000 people in a 375-square-mile area. The FNS dramatically elevated the quality of health care in Leslie County and southeastern Kentucky. The FNS averaged "a baby a day" and had a doctor and

IMPROVING HIS EASTERN KENTUCKY HOMELAND

dentist on staff, as well as a consulting surgeon. The FNS's main hospital was located in Hyden. It was an eighteen-bed, two story stone building completed in 1928.

A patient being carried to the Hyden Hospital before the road was completed. Willie Sandlin in foreground. *Courtesy Ruth Huston*

Hospital in Hyden

On June 26, 1928, the Hyden Hospital of the Frontier Nursing Service was dedicated at an all-day meeting, featuring talks and testimonials by twenty-nine persons "from the principal cities of Kentucky and bordering states." Sir Leslie Mackenzie of Scotland made the dedication address. It was an important and literally life-changing day in the lives of Willie Sandlin and the residents of the rural counties surrounding Hyden. Thousands of families, including the Sandlins, had lost loved ones because of an absence of professional medical care. Mary Breckinridge and the nurses of the Frontier Nursing Service were elevating their quality of life.

The program started at ten in the morning, but the crowd began assembling shortly after daybreak. Persons from distant hills and hollows came in smaller numbers than expected because a constant rain had swollen the Middle Fork and the river was too deep for safe fording. Still, grateful men, women, and children traveled ten to thirty miles from Cutshin, Hell for Certain, Greasy Creek, and other local communities. Some walked and others rode horses or mules, cutting across mountain ridges to avoid swollen streams.

Preceding Sir Leslie on the program, Dr. J. W. Hutchins, President of Berea College, dedicated the new hospital "to the heroes of the impossible – the nurses who have followed Mrs. Breckinridge in this outstanding achievement." Other presenters included C. N. Manning of Lexington, Judge L. D. Lewis of Hyden, E. S. Jouett, a railroad executive, and Mrs. Mary Breckinridge. [3]

* * *

While Breckinridge worked to promote health care in Appalachian Kentucky, Cora Wilson Stewart led a state-wide crusade to promote literacy that began in Morehead, where she began her teaching career in 1895. She quickly earned a reputation as an outstanding educator, and in 1901, long before the women of Rowan County could vote for her, she was elected as the county's school superintendent. She was reelected as school superintendent in 1909 and two years later she became the first woman president of the Kentucky Educational Association.

In 1911, to combat illiteracy in her home county, Mrs. Stewart launched an experimental program – the Moonlight School – which later became a model for adult literacy programs across Kentucky and America. As the leader of Kentucky's anti-illiteracy program, Stewart received the assistance of Kentucky's great war hero, Willie Sandlin. [4] "When I met him, he could hardly read or write," said Mrs. Stewart. "I taught him the multiplication tables myself after the war. He came back from the army aroused to the necessity of an education." However, letters written by Willie Sandlin and the clear recollections of his daughters, Florence and Leona, refute this assessment of Sandlin's literacy. "He could read and write before the war," said Leona. His daughters remember Willie reading *Thousandsticks*, the Hyden newspaper. He also read magazines and completed forms and wrote reports when he was a WPA road supervisor. As part of his work with the WPA, he took a 16-week training course in leadership and personnel management — work which would have required literacy. Sandlin's literacy skills probably improved in the 1920s and 1930s under the tutelage of Cora Wilson Stewart. [5]

Cora Wilson Stewart often commented that the Moonlight Schools took Rowan County "from moonshine and bullets to lemonade and Bibles." *University of Kentucky Library and Archives.*

By 1919, Mrs. Stewart's efforts in Rowan County evolved into the Kentucky Illiteracy Commission. She persuaded "an array of speakers" to take her literacy campaign across the state. For example, on October 3, 1919, Cora Stewart and Willie Sandlin spoke at the court house in Cynthiana, Harrison County. Several weeks later, on October 22, 1919, Mrs. Stewart and Willie Sandlin visited the moonlight schools in and around Bowling Green in Warren County. Speaking to a large delegation of Warren County's moonlight school teachers and students, the visitors declared the moonlight school at Boyce was "the best in Kentucky," with an attendance of seventy pupils. Stewart biographer Yvonne Baldwin wrote that Stewart "found the perfect spokesman, a war hero whose own experiences personified what her crusade was all about." Willie Sandlin supported Mrs. Stewart's efforts because he wanted "to do something to make the people of the

Cora Wilson Stewart, 1913 (above). Stewart's Moonlight Schools advanced the cause of literacy in Kentucky and became a model for national and international literacy campaigns. *Library of Congress.*

The Cora Wilson Stewart Moonlight School is maintained as a tourist attraction in Morehead, Kentucky. It is located near the Rowan County Chamber of Commerce on First Street. *Rowan County Tourism Commission.*

IMPROVING HIS EASTERN KENTUCKY HOMELAND

mountains realize the value of an education." On four separate occasions, Sandlin had refused to accept a battlefield commission because he felt that his limited education would keep him from performing the duties of an officer.

His simple message, made powerful by his experience, stressed the role of parents in keeping children in school. As a child, Sandlin was allowed to remain home from school, he said, and did not realize the value of an education until it was too late. He urged all Kentuckians to learn to read and write and to send the children to school every day. An effective advocate for the Moonlight Schools, Sandlin drew large crowds and converted many to the cause. ⁶

> *Willie Sandlin, "Kentucky's greatest hero" had **joined the crusade "to help stamp out illiteracy in Kentucky."** Sandlin toured Kentucky with Cora Wilson Stewart and spoke in hundreds of towns and villages.*

Newspapers reported that Willie Sandlin, "Kentucky's greatest hero" had joined the crusade "to help stamp out illiteracy in Kentucky." Sandlin toured the state with Stewart and spoke in hundreds of towns and villages. Sandlin was the main speaker when the Kentucky Illiteracy Commission began a ten-week campaign in rural communities. Mrs. Stewart announced that Sergeant Sandlin would "devote all his time to the campaign until its close at which time he will resume his studies at some school or college." With World War I behind him, Sandlin declared "the greatest war" before Kentuckians and Americans was the war to fight illiteracy. Sandlin was quoted as saying that literacy was "the best remedy against Bolshevism and social unrest;" however, that was doubtlessly something that Mrs. Stewart said. He and Mrs. Stewart awarded prizes to the best and most successful moonlight school in the districts they visited, and their efforts often inspired good-spirited competition between counties. For example, after Willie and Mrs. Stewart spoke in Fort Thomas, which was in the "banner county" for literacy in the 1910 census, Campbell County was challenged by

SERGEANT SANDLIN

Robertson County for "first place in the 1920 census." Miss Addie Mae Yeager, the county agent for literacy in Robertson County, had identified all the county illiterates and had encouraged "half of them" to attend the county's moonlight school. Rising to the challenge, Campbell County, which already had a much lower literacy rate – 1.9% compared to 8.9% – raised $500 to purchase books for adult illiterates, and the town of Alexandria, inspired by Sandlin and Stewart, planned "to have the largest moonlight school in the state."

In November 1919, Mrs. Stewart and Sergeant Sandlin spent several days in Laurel County, speaking at five schools each day, "to stimulate interest in the eradication of illiteracy by 1920." E.B. Wolf, the county illiteracy agent, introduced the speakers. Sergeant Sandlin told about some of his war experiences that prompted him to seek more education for himself and to join the fight against illiteracy in his home state. Mrs. Stewart followed with a discussion of how the moonlight school program for adult illiterates was earning state and national recognition for its success. Mr. Wolf concluded with a report that Laurel County was working hard to promote day school attendance. "Keep the children in school to prevent future illiteracy," was his slogan. 7

Cora Wilson Stewart first opened her schools to adults during mooonlit evenings in the winter of 1911. *Kentucky Department of Library and Archives.*

Sandlin was so dedicated to Mrs. Stewart's campaign that he and Belvia named their second child after her – Cora Wilson Stewart Sandlin – and they developed a friendship with the nationally famous champion of literacy. Mrs.

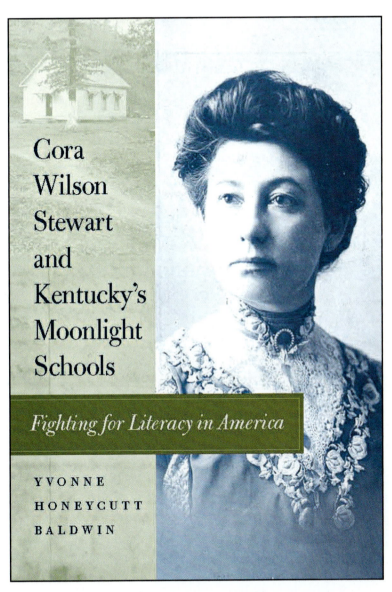

Yvonne Honeycutt Baldwin, now a retired Professor in the History Department at Morehead State University, produced an excellent book that examines Stewart's life and her philosophy of teaching adult illiterates. *Courtesy of The University Press of Kentucky.*

Cora Wilson Stewart wrote reading primers for classroom use that provided practical lessons about everyday life. She designed reading books for rural people, soldiers, Native Americans, prisoners, and mothers. *University of Kentucky Library and Archives.*

Stewart often acted as a scribe and secretary for Kentucky's illiterates. In 1921, she had directed a letter on Sandlin's behalf seeking a duplicate of the Montenegrin War Cross which Sandlin had lost or misplaced. By the time Mrs. Stewart's letter arrived at the Legation of the Kingdom of the Serbs, Croats, and Slovenes in Washington, DC, the Kingdom of Montenegro no longer existed and the Legation was "unable to comply" with her request. [8]

By the mid-1920s, the friendship between the Sandlins and Cora Wilson Stewart had grown even stronger. Mrs. Stewart had visited the Sandlin home and the Sergeant and his wife thanked her for her visit and wished she "could have stayed a week or longer." Belvia shared information about her family's health and activities. Little Cora had been sick "with the same trouble Vorres had – tonsils." Mrs. Stewart had given Cora a present that she proudly showed to all visitors.

A month later, Belvia shared the tragic news of her daughter Cora's death. "She died the second day of Oct. You know we sure hated to give her up but God can call any of them away." Mrs. Stewart had taken a photograph of her namesake and Belvia wanted a copy of the picture. Vorres was not well, but "the baby was fine," reported the distressed mother.

A persistent theme in the Belvia Sandlin/Cora Wilson Stewart correspondence was Willie's pension. "The Sergeant" was only getting $10.50 a month and commented that he was like the Kaiser: "the Kiser didn't have any friends and [Willie didn't] have any pension." Willie felt that his politics worked against him. He was a Democrat and felt that "Republicans don't like to give to Democrats." And the Bureaus, he thought, were "all Republican." "Sergeant appreciates any thing you could do regarding his pension," Belvia concluded. A month later, Belvia wrote about needing more money in "the Sergeant's" pension. Mrs. Stewart had offered to write on Willie's behalf and Belvia encouraged her to "publish any thing you wish to about him."

Rural communities around the state rose to Cora Wilson Stewart's literacy challenge. In Leslie County, Sandlin's home county, teachers challenged their communities to teach illiterates to read and write in an effort to rid the state of illiteracy by March 1920. In September, with the "bean picking, sorghum making and fodder pulling" complete, teachers vowed to begin their moonlight schools with renewed enthusiasm and work until "every man and woman in Leslie County can read and write." In 1920, Leslie County had "more illiterates than any county in Kentucky" and teachers rose to the challenge presented by Cora Wilson Stewart and Willie Sandlin to "clear the county of illiterates."[9]

In her book, *Moonlight Schools*, Stewart observed that many soldiers returned from WWI with an increased awareness of the need for literacy. It was, she observed, "the burden of every soldier's heart." In his public testimonials,

SERGEANT SANDLIN

Sergeant Sandlin told "of the many commissions offered him in France" which he had declined because of his limited education. Mrs. Stewart observed that Sandlin's remarks had a "crude but eloquent appeal." [10]

Years later, when World War II began, illiterates were still not accepted into the Army. The famous war hero, Alvin York, sought permission to "lead a battalion of [Appalachia's] rejected youths." Commenting on more than 8000 illiterate Kentuckians and Tennesseans who had been rejected, York proclaimed: "They are crack shots and they know how to handle themselves and they can endure hardships. They are the best soldiers in the world." York and Willie Sandlin, along with many others, denounced this policy as shortsighted and unimaginative: "It is not half so difficult to teach young men to read and write as it is to teach them to be good soldiers." In 1942, the *Louisville Courier Journal* joined this crusade and urged the army to accept illiterates and teach them to read "before their formal induction." "Their country owes them that much even if it never needed them for soldiers. But it does need them which should be a double incentive to solve the problem they present as quickly and as simply as possible." [11]

Learning that the Sandlins had surrendered their rented farm and moved in with his wife's family at the mouth of Owl's Nest Creek, Cora Wilson Stewart remarked that it was "a disgrace to Kentucky" that Sandlin and his family had lived in a two-room cabin on a rented farm. "They're out now," she observed, "and Willie Sandlin doesn't have a roof of his own to shelter his wife and their three little daughters." Stewart's well-intentioned concern for Willie Sandlin, combined with several sensationalized newspaper articles from beyond Appalachia, did not overstate his financial despair and ill health. However, Sandlin, ever the loving and dutiful father, hid his problems from his children. His youngest daughter Florence remembered "Dad was always working and had enough to help others in the county." [12]

In the fell clutch of circumstance
I have not winced nor cried aloud.
Under the bludgeonings of chance
My head is bloody, but unbowed.
"Invictus"
William Ernest Henley

CHAPTER SIX
NO VETERANS BENEFITS FOR AN INJURED HERO, 1921-1933

Willie Sandlin was discharged from the army in 1919. Like all veterans, he received $60, a train ticket home, and the promise of a $500 bonus to be paid in the future. By the end of the war, 4.7 million Americans had served; 116,000 were killed, and 204,000, like Sandlin, had been wounded. Willie had been gassed twice in the Argonne Forest and he had a bullet wound in his head and a fragment wound in his leg. Like 204,000 others, Sandlin was eligible for benefits because of his injuries. [1]

Veterans benefits was a well-established concept long before America's entry into World War I. As early as 1636, the Plymouth Colony enacted a law to provide benefits to disabled veterans of conflicts with the Pequot Indians. In 1776, the Continental Congress passed the first pension law as a way to increase military enlistments; disabled veterans could receive half-pay for life. However, because of limited federal resources, the states were responsible for paying benefits, so many veterans never received any payments.

By 1808, veterans benefits were administered by the Secretary of War's

SERGEANT SANDLIN

Bureau of Pensions. Three years later, the first veterans medical facility was authorized, but the construction was not completed until 1833.

By the early years of the Civil War, the federal government had established a pension payment system. After the Civil War, veterans homes were established and served as residences and health care facilities for indigent and disabled veterans of all previous conflicts, including those who did not serve in a combat area. Union veterans were provided pensions based on rank and disability. Confederate veterans were excluded until 1958 when Congress pardoned them and extended benefits to the single remaining survivor. Civil War veteran benefits peaked in 1913 when veteran benefits accounted for about one-third of the total federal budget. Because of these high costs, the public tended to oppose veteran benefits in general.

> *Shortly after Sandlin's discharge from the army, the public became aware of his health problems.* **Ever the loving father, Willie Sandlin hid his pain and illness from his children**. *When the children were little, they thought their father was in good health because he was constantly working to support his large family.*

Sandlin and his fellow injured veterans returned home to a nation that had authorized new protocols for awarding benefits to veterans. New benefits included disability compensation, vocational rehabilitation for the disabled, and insurance for active-duty personnel and veterans. Three agencies were formed: the Veterans Bureau, the Bureau of Pensions, and the National Home for Disabled Volunteer Soldiers. The agencies were administered by the War Department.

Shortly after Sandlin's discharge from the army, the public became aware of his health problems. Ever the loving father, Willie hid his pain and illness from his children. When the children were little, they thought their father was

NO VETERAN'S BENEFITS FOR AN INJURED HERO

in good health because he was constantly working to support his large family. However, after Willie died, Belvia told her children that Willie often had trouble breathing at night, and he would get out of bed and go downstairs and sit with his back against the chimney all night. The heat apparently provided some relief. Although Willie often got little sleep, he got up the next morning, helped his children get ready for school, and went to work. [2]

When Willie first came home from the war, a large crowd gathered at the Leslie County Court House to welcome "one of forty-seven of the greatest heroes of the war." They felt that Willie had brought great honor to their county and saw him as a "typical son of the mountains." [3]

Aware of the gifts that Tennesseans had bestowed on Alvin York, "their mountain hero," Judge John C. Eversole suggested that Kentuckians buy a farm for Willie Sandlin "so as not to be outdone by the citizens of Tennessee." A local fundraising committee was appointed and Judge Eversole was empowered to appoint "similar committees" in neighboring counties. All Kentuckians were encouraged to contribute to this worthy project and make or send their contributions to Judge Eversole or to J. H. Asher in nearly Hyden. The honored guest, Medal of Honor recipient Willie Sandlin made a few remarks and "consented to accept anything that his fellow citizens could do for him." [4]

After hearing speeches by other local politicians, attendees were told that Sergeant Sandlin and other local veterans of the Great War would receive further recognition during a July 4th "basket picnic at the mouth of Hurt's Creek." The picnic featured "splendid military discussions" by Lieutenant Claiborne Fetner. Attendees were advised that no "special trains" would run for the occasions but there would be "plenty of mules available after the crops are laid by." The Fourth of July celebration would be an opportunity for people with "loyal hearts" to show "real pride in what our humble mountain lads have done to protect freedom on the earth." [5]

SERGEANT SANDLIN

Willie Was Gassed

During World War I, for the first time in the history of warfare, deadly gases were used as weapons. The gases the German army used burned the skin and damaged the nose, throat, and lungs of Allied soldiers. The gas was so lethal that it could cause death or paralysis within minutes. American soldiers learned how to use a gas mask before they went overseas. When they arrived in Europe, some were assigned to European units, and English and French officers routinely took their new American support troops into the trenches for a more detailed explanation of the use of their gas masks. While fighting from the trenches, Sandlin and his fellow soldiers would be warned of a gas attack by a whistle, alarm bell, or shouted alert. At that point, soldiers donned their protective masks or hoods as quickly as possible, a skill that became a necessary part of survival for a soldier on the front lines. Soldiers who were gassed were normally sent to medical units where they bathed and put on clean clothes, but that was not always possible. When Willie Sandlin was gassed, he refused to leave his platoon to seek medical assistance. Like many others who were exposed to the poison gas used by the German army, Sandlin suffered the painful and debilitating effects of damaged lungs until he died.

The German High Command sanctioned the use of gas – as did the Allies – hoping that chemical weapons would break the lengthy stalemate of trench

Postcard with image of gas attack. *National World War I Museum and Memorial, Kansas City, Missouri.*

warfare and lead to decisive victory. By the end of World War I, the use of chemical gas had resulted in more than 1.3 million injuries and approximately 90,000 deaths. In addition to those who suffered injury or death, a large number of soldiers, munitions workers, and civilians suffered psychological damage from "gas fright," which left many soldiers with uncontrollable tremors known as "shell shock." Known as "soldiers' heart" in the American Civil War and "combat fatigue" during World War II, shell shock was the forerunner of today's post-traumatic stress disorder. Thousands more, like Willie Sandlin, died from gas exposure during the 1920s, 1930, and 1940s. After World War I ended, deadly gases as weapons of war were banned, although many American and Vietnamese soldiers later suffered from exposure to chemical agents during the Vietnam War.

When the American soldiers entered the war in 1917, the army did not have an established medical corps. Their developing medical corps copied the processes of the British and French armies, and the U.S. medical efforts were supplemented by the brave and able assistance of Red Cross nurses, who often worked fourteen-hour days in base hospitals or evacuation hospitals. These evac hospitals were often within eight to ten miles of the front lines, certainly within the range of German artillery.

If Willie Sandlin had left his platoon to seek medical assistance, the effects of being gassed might have been less severe. Further, if Sandlin had sought medical assistance, that fact would have been made a part of his military records, and he might have received disability funds from the Veterans Bureau. [6]

Willie Pursues Disability Benefits

Like many wounded veterans, Sandlin wasted no time in pursuing benefits. In 1921, government physicians at a Veterans Center in Richmond, Kentucky, examined Sandlin and reported that he was "suffering a serious lung infection as a result of gas inhaled" in the Battle of the Argonne Forest. A "full report" of his condition went to the national office in Washington "for action."

Soldiers who received this citation during World War I could apply for the Purple Heart award when it was created in 1932. *Florence Muncy Collection.*

However, no assistance was forthcoming from any government agencies. [7]

Two years earlier, in 1919 the American Legion had been founded by WWI veterans. It quickly became a powerful and effective advocate for improvements to the veterans' hospital system. In the early 1920s, shell-shocked veterans were being treated in medical facilities for "feeble minded" children, because no other facilities existed to treat America's shell-shocked veterans. Lobbying by the American Legion led to increased funding for much-needed medical care for some veterans, but none was forthcoming for Willie Sandlin, one of the true heroes of the Great War. [8]

On May 19, 1924, Congress passed the World War Adjusted Compensation Act which awarded veterans additional pay in various forms. The value of each veteran's "credit" was based on each recipient's service between April 5, 1917, and July 1, 1919, with $1 awarded for each day served in the United States (maximum payment of $500) and $1.25 for each day served abroad (maximum of $625). Most officers and those whose service began after November 11, 1918, (Armistice Day) were excluded. Immediate payments were made to those due less than $50; the estate of a deceased veteran was paid immediately if the amount was less than $500. All others were awarded an "Adjusted Service Certificate," a "bonus" which functioned like an insurance policy; the value was based on the value of a 20-year policy equal to 125% of the service credit. The veteran's Certificate was to be awarded on his first birthday after January 1, 1925, and could be redeemed in full on his birthday in 1945, with payments made to estates of veterans who died before 1945. Certificates could be used as loan collateral in some circumstances. President Coolidge vetoed the bill, but the Senate overrode his decision. After the war, Sandlin had received $40 a month from the government, but that was cut to $10 per month by the Veterans Bureau in 1923. Sandlin still had nothing from Uncle Sam except $10 per month for receiving the Medal of Honor. [9]

In 1925, in order to make a claim for increased compensation, Sandlin was in Lexington to appear before the United States Veterans' Bureau. Sandlin was

NO VETERAN'S BENEFITS FOR AN INJURED HERO

still only receiving $10 a month. The Hugh McKee Post of the VFW had filed an appeal on Sandlin's behalf to "have his former allowance restored." On July 4, 1924, Sandlin had been initiated into the McKee Post, "the most decorated organization in the world." The State Commander of the VFW was, at that time, Captain Robert E. Lee Murphy, a member of the Hugh McKee Post. Murphy had served in World War I with Lieutenant Leigh Wade, one of the Around-the-World Fliers. Murphy had been wounded in action, cited for gallantry, and had shot down three enemy planes. [10]

Robert E. Lee Murphy

Robert E. Lee Murphy was a friend to Willie Sandlin for many years. In the two decades after the Great War ended, Murphy devoted much energy to raising money to purchase a home for Sandlin. However, Sandlin never received a penny of this "Hero Fund," and his children later maintained that Murphy "stole Daddy's money."

Robert Murphy's father, Cornelius Walter Murphy, came to America from Cork, Ireland, when he was a young man. He made a number of trips back to Ireland before settling in Virginia during the antebellum period. Murphy served under Robert E. Lee during the Civil War. After the war, he married Lydia Beaumont Dunn and lived in Garrard County, Virginia, for many years. In 1913, the Murphys moved to Lexington, Kentucky.

His son, R.E.L. Murphy, worked his way through Berea College and later completed the four-year law course at the University of Kentucky in two years. He was an attorney and member of the Fayette County Bar Association when America entered World War I. Murphy joined the army in 1917 and trained at the officers' training camp at Fort Benjamin Harrison. There he was selected as one of twenty-five men to be trained in aviation by the English Royal Air Force Service in Canada. He was later attached to the Royal Air Force. After further training, he became a bomber pilot until the end of the war. As a bomber pilot,

SERGEANT SANDLIN

> **Robert E. Lee Murphy was a successful lawyer and politician who once attempted to run for governor**, and a *controversial champion of veterans' rights and benefits who played a leadership role in state and national veterans organizations.*

---

his plane was twice forced down in enemy territory by engine trouble, but both times he made his way back to Allied lines. Transferred to scout planes, he was struck by antiaircraft fire at 3000 feet, but managed to land his disabled plane in American-held territory. When fighting ended, Murphy was sent to Paris as a member of the legal department of the American Peace Commission, remaining there until the peace treaty was concluded.

Murphy returned to the States in April 1919 and spent two and half months in the Aviation Convalescent Hospital in Cooperstown, New Jersey, recovering from "his machine being put out of commission 13,000 feet above the German lines" during the Argonne offensive. He then returned to Lexington where his name "attested to the loyalty of his parents as well as himself to the Democratic party." Murphy, who had been admitted to the Kentucky State Bar in 1914, was licensed to practice before the U.S. Supreme Court in 1920.

Murphy married Lucile Louise Antin of Paris, France, on May 25, 1926, in Louisville, Kentucky. The young couple then spent several weeks in Paris before sailing from Marseilles, France, to Buenos Aires, Argentina, where they spent several months. The couple first met when Captain Murphy was serving as an aviator in France, first with the Royal Air Force and later with the American Air Service.

Like many World War I veterans, Murphy led an interesting life. Prior to his law study, Murphy worked as a clown in a circus and as a cowboy on western ranches. In later years, he annually promoted the selection of a "Miss Kentucky"

NO VETERAN'S BENEFITS FOR AN INJURED HERO

to take part in the Atlantic City beauty contest.

For the remainder of his career, Murphy was a successful lawyer and politician who once attempted to run for governor, and a controversial champion of veterans' rights and benefits who played a leadership role in state and national veterans organizations. [11]

* * *

By the fall of 1925, Mr. Murphy and other members of the McKee Post intensified their efforts to secure more financial recompense for Willie Sandlin. Sandlin was the "heroest hero" of the Great War, according to newspaper reports. "He accumulated enough glory in one day to chalk off all the valorous deeds of most heroes and have enough left for ordinary citation purposes." [12] Speaking at the national VFW convention in Lexington, Murphy declared: "Kentucky, since the war, holds the record for doing less for her veterans than any other state in the Union," and Murphy cited examples of other war heroes who had received generous support from their home state. Murphy criticized the priorities of the state government and then asked the convention to "endorse a campaign . . . to buy Sergeant Willie Sandlin a home in Leslie County." [13]

After that, heated conflict developed between the VFW and the state government. In December 1925, the VFW went on record as "opposing further appropriations" to the Kentucky Ex-Service Men's Board at Louisville and charged that this state-supported office "had squandered $50,000 in four years." VFW resolutions charged that the entire $50,000 had been "wasted and squandered by the three members of the board and the secretary" and that no disabled veteran had benefitted from the $50,000 expenditures. Adding fuel to the fire, the VFW charged that no member of the board nor the secretary "had ever been wounded or disabled and knew nothing of the needs of disabled veterans."

The VFW council called for greater patriotism in Kentucky and decided to take "immediate steps" to initiate their campaign to raise $10,000 to buy a home

SERGEANT SANDLIN

for Kentucky's only native World War I Medal of Honor recipient, who now, they proclaimed, was only receiving $10 a month from the government although he had been wounded and gassed during the war. [14]

Within a month of these declarations by the VFW, Governor William J. Fields agreed to head a committee of "100 prominent Kentuckians" who would support the VFW campaign to raise $10,000 to buy a home and farm in Leslie County for Willie Sandlin. Included on the committee with the Governor were U.S. Senator Richard P. Ernst; Hon. John M. Robison, Congressman from the 11th District, in which Willie Sandlin resided; Mrs. Peter J. Campbell, President of Kentucky War Mothers; Mrs. Elizabeth A. Ray, State Regent, Kentucky Daughters of the American Revolution (DAR); Irvin S. Cobb, world famed humorist; D. W. Griffith, movie producer; and Mrs. Cora Wilson Stewart, known throughout the world for her work in establishing "moonlight schools;" and many others. [15] The campaign began in January 1926 with a $100 gift from Joe H. Smith, a central Kentucky farmer. The names of donors were to be filed with the Secretary of State's office in Frankfort and copies of all documents were to be sent to the Sandlins and to the VFW post in Lexington.

Meanwhile, Murphy planned to enlist the assistance of the National Commander of the VFW for his friend Willie Sandlin who could not, according to Murphy, "support his wife and two babies." By the end of January 1926, the "Hero Fund" had been endorsed by the DAR and the State War Mothers. The VFW, which had already raised $1000 in Lexington, was planning "an intensive drive in Louisville to put the fund over the top." [16]

The following month, Sandlin's claims of inadequate compensation were publicly challenged by state officials. Colonel F. M. Roark, regional manager of the Veterans Bureau, speaking at an American Legion luncheon, said that Sandlin's claim "was not borne out by the records." Roark argued that Sandlin's military records contained "no mention of Sandlin having been gassed, wounded or hospitalized at any time." Supporting Roark's claims, James D. Story, Jr.,

NO VETERAN'S BENEFITS FOR AN INJURED HERO

> *Sandlin's claim of inadequate compensation were publicly challenged by state officials.* **Colonel F. M. Roark, regional manager of the Veterans Bureau, speaking at an American Legion luncheon, said that Sandlin's claim "was not borne out by the records."** *Roark argued that Sandlin's military records contained "no mention of Sandlin having been gassed, wounded or hospitalized at any time."*

secretary of the Ex-Service Men's Board, noted that Sandlin had been offered transportation to Louisville and served with notice to appear before the rating board, but "he has not come." [17]

At that point, the battle of accusations devolved into open warfare. The VFW countered by sending postcards to each member of the Kentucky House of Representatives inviting legislators to attend a "mass meeting" at the Lexington Court House on the evening of Wednesday, February 17, 1926. Representative Fowler of Louisville introduced a motion asking the Speaker to appoint a five-person committee to attend the meeting and listen to the VFW grievances. Because the state had invested $15,000 in the work of the Veterans Bureau, the motion passed because legislators argued the VFW charges should be investigated. The House committee included Representatives Leslie, Seale, Berry, Holbrook, and Fowler, who was a member of the Jefferson Post of the American Legion and knowledgeable of veterans' issues in Kentucky. In addition to attending the VFW meeting, Fowler's committee was empowered to "summon witnesses and hear evidence." In preparation for the mass meeting, R.E.L. Murphy, the principal speaker, announced that "checks have been stolen, compensation denied, false statements filed in the Veterans Bureau regarding disabled veterans, and an attempt has been made to dishonor

SERGEANT SANDLIN

> *Through no intention of his own,* **Willie Sandlin had become the central figure in a firestorm of conflict** *regarding the compensation of Kentucky's veterans.*

Sergeant Willie Sandlin, the greatest American hero."

These charges and other "astounding facts" were to be revealed by the VFW at their mass meeting in Lexington. Through no intention of his own, Willie Sandlin had become the central figure in a firestorm of conflict regarding the compensation of Kentucky's veterans. The mass meeting in Lexington featured hostile discussions between Murphy, who convened the meeting, and Fowler, a representative of the state government. At first Murphy refused to allow Fowler to speak. Finally, after much heated debate, Fowler stated that "any veteran who feels or knows his claim has not received proper consideration is invited to appear before the Military Affairs Committee of the House," a committee empowered "to see that veterans be given justice." That same week, Murphy defended Sandlin's compensation claim at the American Legion Luncheon Club in Louisville. Denouncing the Veterans Bureau explanation that Sandlin's records showed no evidence of injury or being gassed, Murphy rightfully argued that there "were hundreds of men wounded during the war whose wounds do not appear on their records." [18]

A month later, Fowler's committee, the House Committee on Military Affairs, presented a formal report to the state House of Representatives on the VFW charges that had been made at the Lexington meeting. The committee denounced the Lexington mass meeting for "malicious intent, without any basis in fact," to discredit the United States Veterans Bureau and the Kentucky Disabled Ex-Service Men's Bureau. Chairman Fowler and his committee

NO VETERAN'S BENEFITS FOR AN INJURED HERO

unanimously condemned Robert E. Lee Murphy as self-promotional and a

> *malignant liar, a disgrace to the uniform of his country, to Kentucky, to America and to the Veterans of Foreign Wars of which he is the self-perpetuated State Commander.*

The committee report, accepted and adopted by the House of Representatives, said that "the most charitable thing that could be said of Murphy is that he is insane." Further, the committee recommended that their report be turned over to the Department of Justice for "further investigation" of potential wrongdoing by Murphy, who was, in the committee's opinion, telling "malignant lies to discredit worthy bureaus." [19]

At the Lexington mass meeting, six ex-servicemen testified that they had been badly treated and that they had been denied compensation. These six men along with Murphy, were summoned to testify before the House Committee on Military Affairs and they failed to appear. The committee denounced Murphy for arguing that Sandlin had been unfairly treated. "Sandlin was not present at the [mass] meeting, nor did he send anyone nor any statements to be read on his behalf," so the House Committee on Military Affairs judged that Murphy had either overstated or mispresented Sandlin's case. The House committee argued that Sandlin had not appeared for examination by the Veterans Bureau, and Murphy admitted at the Lexington mass meeting "that he had advised Sergeant Sandlin not to appear for examination."

Murphy's plan to have the House Committee on Military Affairs intervene on behalf of Sandlin and other veterans had failed. The committee denounced Murphy's "malicious attempt" to discredit the Veterans Bureau. Murphy, according to the House Committee "was refused further membership in Lexington Post No. 8 of the American Legion" and was "banished from a national organization." The committee further concluded that Murphy was using his influence over "all agencies under his control for the furtherance of his private and personal interests." Sadly, for Willie Sandlin, the wrong person had championed his cause and it is certainly possible that Sandlin's association with Murphy might have worked against his efforts to receive additional veterans benefits. [20]

Despite the setbacks caused by the House Committee's denunciation of Murphy, the Lexington attorney continued his campaign to raise funds for the purpose of purchasing a farm and home for Sergeant Willie Sandlin. For that reason, it was difficult for Sandlin to disassociate himself from Murphy. So the fundraising continued with the support of several patriotic organizations and many of the state's prominent citizens. In May, 1927, for example, at a regularly scheduled meeting in Lexington of the Kentucky chapter of the DAV, a resolution was adopted to be forwarded to General Frank T. Hines, director of the United States Veterans Bureau in Washington, D.C., "requesting that Sergeant Willie Sandlin . . . be ordered to Cincinnati at once for an examination to have his compensation reinstated." In June, the Lexington chapter had received more than 500 letters from disabled veterans in Kentucky "asking for assistance." The Lexington chapter of the DAV working in conjunction with a recently opened state office pledged to "give assistance to all disabled veterans in the state" and Willie Sandlin was the poster boy. [21]

In June 1927, the VFW held their state convention of Disabled American War Veterans at the Phoenix Hotel in Lexington. Among the officers elected at the convention were State Commander R. E. L. Murphy of Lexington and Chief of Staff Sergeant Willie Sandlin of Leslie County. The convention voted to incorporate and to establish permanent state headquarters in Lexington. Murphy was selected to represent Kentucky's disabled veterans at the national convention held in El Paso, Texas, the following week. At the closing session of the state meeting, the disabled veterans approved resolutions

> *demanding better service by the Veterans' Bureau to disabled veterans, favoring a $10-a-month bonus to World War veterans, favoring an unlimited extension of the time for filing veterans'*

NO VETERAN'S BENEFITS FOR AN INJURED HERO

Sandlin's financial despair was well known throughout Leslie county. For about a year after the war, the government had paid him $40 a month. Then his allotment was reduced and finally abolished. **His Medal of Honor entitled him to $10 a month. By 1928 he was getting nothing else**.

---

compensation claims, opposing further extension of the Kentucky Disabled Ex-Service Men's Board, demanding the prosecution of F. M. Roark, former manager of the bureau, and deploring treatment afforded Sergt. Willie Sandlin by the bureau. [22]

Two weeks later, Kentucky's VFW held a meeting at the Combs Hotel in Hazard. At the morning session, the veterans elected officers and then listened to several speakers at a noon luncheon. At the conclusion of the luncheon meeting, the group discussed the fund of $10,000 "to buy a home for Willie Sandlin" and plans for a campaign to increase "the $1200 already raised" were adopted. [23]

Sandlin's financial despair was well known throughout Leslie County. "Well, Willie, have you got your compensation yet?" his friends asked as he walked through the little town of Hyden. It was no laughing matter to Sandlin who had been hoping for financial assistance for six years, but Willie managed to grin and say, "Not yet. Uncle Sam is good pay, but some of his men aren't so fast in writing out the checks." [24] For about a year after the war, the government had paid him $40 a month. Then his allotment was reduced and finally abolished. His Medal of Honor entitled him to $10 a month. By 1928 he was getting nothing else.

131

SERGEANT SANDLIN

On April 9, 1928, Mr. Robinson of Indiana introduced the following bill which was read twice and referred to the Committee on Military Affairs.

70TH CONGRESS
1ST SESSION

S. 3967

IN THE SENATE OF THE UNITED STATES

APRIL 9, 1928

Mr. ROBINSON of Indiana introduced the following bill; which was read twice and referred to the Committee on Military Affairs

---

A BILL

For the relief of Willie Sandlin.

1 *Be it enacted by the Senate and House of Representa-*
2 *tives of the United States of America in Congress assembled,*
3 That the President of the United States be, and he is hereby,
4 authorized and empowered to appoint, by and with the
5 advice and consent of the Senate, Willie Sandlin, formerly
6 sergeant in the Regular Army, reenlisted in Company A,
7 One hundred and thirty-second Infantry, United States
8 Army, during the World War, to the position and rank of
9 captain in said Army, with the same pay and upon the same
10 conditions as other retired officers of said grade and rank
11 receive.

NO VETERAN'S BENEFITS FOR AN INJURED HERO

The bill never left the Committee on Military Affairs and the United States Senate took no further action on behalf of Sergeant Willie Sandlin.

Apparently dissatisfied with the VFW's efforts to secure benefits for veterans, Murphy and Sandlin created a new veterans organization. In the fall of 1928, the American War Veterans filed Articles of Incorporation with the Secretary of State in Frankfort. Willie Sandlin's name headed a list of distinguished Kentuckians who signed the Articles. One of the stated objects of the organization was to secure pensions for all disabled Word War veterans "regardless of service connection'" and also pensions of "not less than $50 per month" for disabled veterans of the Spanish-American War and the Philippine Insurrection who were at least 50 years old. The incorporators stated that there were more than "500,000 Disabled Veterans of the World War who are not receiving compensation." Sandlin and Murphy were among the new organization's elected officers.

Soon other states were organizing and chartering posts of the American War Veterans. In Helena, Montana, the Woodrow Wilson Post included 195 charter members, "all patients at the United States veterans' hospital." In December 1928, the Woodrow Wilson Post elected officers in the local post of a fledgling national organization that was "unique in that veterans of any war are eligible to membership including soldiers of the Confederate Army." [25]

While Murphy and Sandlin were attempting to energize the American War Veterans, they remained active in the VFW, which held its national convention in Louisville in September 1929. Almost 4000 war veterans arrived by plane, train, boat, and automobile. Sergeant Alvin York, Lieutenant Samuel Woodfill, and Sergeant Willie Sandlin, three of the "outstanding heroes" of World War I, notified VFW national headquarters of their plans to attend.

Sandlin was faced with the possibility of not being able to attend because he did not have a uniform. He wanted to be present at the Louisville meeting "and talk over old times with his buddies." When Sandlin's plight was reported to Kentucky Governor Flem D. Sampson, the Governor summoned the Adjutant

Sergeant Alvin York was America's best-known hero of the First World War. Like Willie Sandlin, he remained a quiet and assuming person in his civilian life. *National Archives.*

NO VETERAN'S BENEFITS FOR AN INJURED HERO

General of the Kentucky National Guard and instructed him to requisition a new uniform for Sandlin. Sandlin, wearing his new uniform, and the other distinguished guests were assigned military aides and were treated with great courtesy and respect. [26]

In 1928, at age 38, Sandlin should have been in his physical prime when he moved back to the "weaning house," but instead, according to some newspaper accounts, he was very ill. Sandlin "coughed and wheezed a great deal," especially in the winter. By 1928, Sandlin had spent time in hospitals in Chillicothe, Ohio, Cincinnati, and "other places." An old army buddy encouraged Willie to move to Colorado because he thought "the dry air and high altitude" would help him. But Willie would not leave his eastern Kentucky homeland, and he didn't have enough money to travel if he had wanted to. "I'm not one-third the man I used to be before the war," he observed without complaint. "If I take 25 steps up the hill, I'm done for. My wind's gone." Willie believed the German poison gas had made him cough and wheeze and kept him in bed half the winter. In 1928, the VFW reported that German shot, shell, and poison gas had transformed Willie into a "physical wreck" and the government awarded him with a "pitifully inadequate allowance of $10 per month" to support his family. That same year, Senator Hiram Brock's bill to appropriate $10,000 to purchase a farm for war hero Willie Sandlin "was reported favorably by the Senate Committee on Appropriations." Also, in 1928 Senator R. Robinson and others presented a bill to Congress which "would enlist and retire as a captain Willie Sandlin, Kentucky hero of the world war, who is now destitute." [27]

Hiram Brock

Hiram Brock played an important role in Kentucky politics for more than three decades. If anyone could have secured state funds for war hero Willie Sandlin, it would have been Brock, who was a hard man to ignore. With his flaming red ties, his imperious manner, and his loud, oratorical voice, "the

Eastern Kentucky University Board of Regents; Hiram Brock, right. *From EKU Special Collections & Archives.*

gentleman from Harlan" made his presence felt in the General Assembly.

Brock, who was born in the late 1870s, was a state legislator when America entered World War I. At age 40, he presented himself at Fort Benjamin Harrison in Louisville seeking admission to the Officers' Reserve Corps.

"I've always wanted to be in the army," Brock said, while staying at Louisville's Watterson Hotel. "In fact, I ran away from home when I was 18 years old and tried to enlist, but was turned down because of my age." "I think I've got a chance now," the 40-year-old lawyer and lawmaker observed. "I'm willing and want to do everything I can." Brock had poor vision, but he was "sound as a dollar, otherwise." Brock had been a member of the Special Tax Commission that drafted new revenue laws for Kentucky.

For thirty-five years, Brock was involved in state politics as a representative, senator, board member, judge, or county attorney in Harlan. In

NO VETERAN'S BENEFITS FOR AN INJURED HERO

his political career, he helped pass Kentucky's first free textbook bill, promoted state highway construction, helped to sponsor the state's first election reform law, and played a key role in establishing Cumberland Falls as a state park.

Brock was a great friend to education. He began his career of public service in 1904 when he was elected to serve as the School Superintendent of Leslie County. He also served 16 years on the Board of Regents at Eastern Kentucky University, which later named the school auditorium in his honor.

Brock was a great man and a devoted public servant who "campaigned over tortuous mountain roads and lashed opponents in letters to the editor." He was a man of vision and accomplishment, but he did not succeed in getting $10,000 from the state legislature for Willie Sandlin. He died in 1963 at age 85. [28]

* * *

Life after the war had been one examination after another for Willie. Late in 1927, he was examined in Cincinnati and given a 69 percent disability rating, which would have entitled him to fair compensation. But the Louisville Veterans Bureau – with jurisdiction over Sandlin – appealed that rating to the Bureau of Appeal in Chicago, which, in turn, placed Sandlin's case before the Veteran's Bureau in Washington. Technicalities blocked Sandlin's appeal for compensation and knowledgeable observers felt that "special action by Congress may be necessary." [29]

The whole process had become exhaustive and demoralizing to Willie Sandlin, yet he had no choice but to continue. The Kentucky Department of the VFW held a two-day encampment at the Jefferson County Armory in July 1928 and the veterans once again pledged to raise the $10,000 to purchase a home for Sandlin. The attendees then adjourned to enjoy a buffet luncheon provided by the ladies auxiliary of the Louisville post and the War Mothers. After lunch, the veterans journeyed to Parkway Field to see the Louisville Colonels baseball team in action. [30]

In 1929, Sandlin's financial problems were intensified by the stock market

Luxury items, which symbolized the 1920s, had to be sacrificed as Americans became mired in the Great Depression. By the end of the Depression, Roosevelt's New Deal programs had alleviated some of the financial misery of both urban and rural Americans. By 1939, Public Works projects had been instituted in all but three counties of the United States. *National Archives.*

NO VETERAN'S BENEFITS FOR AN INJURED HERO

crash and the beginning of the Great Depression, which had a devastating effect upon central and southern Appalachia. By 1933, one-third of the nation's workforce was unemployed and the annual per capita income throughout the South dropped from "a national low of $372 in 1929 to just $203 in 1932." For Sandlin and his Appalachian neighbors, who often commented that they "were already depressed," the depression bred fear, insecurity, hunger, homelessness, and disease. During these hard times, Sandlin continued to support his friends and neighbors and present a positive image to the public. In the fall of 1929, for example, the Leslie County public schools hosted a fair, which included "old fashioned spelling bees" and other school exhibits. At the fair, the 149th Infantry of the Kentucky National Guard, stationed at Hazard, demonstrated military machine guns. During the demonstration, nearby woods were ignited by the tracer bullets, "but little damage resulted." One of the "interested spectators" at the machine gun demonstration was Willie Sandlin. [31]

Bonus Army

In the years following World War I, Congress had passed legislation that would pay Sandlin and all veterans of the conflict an adjusted "bonus" compensation for their time in the service, to be paid out in 1945. However, when the Great Depression struck, many veterans were out of work and wanted the government to pay them immediately rather than in 1945.

Starting in May 1932, veterans from across the country made their way to Washington, DC, to lobby and show their support for a bill introduced in Congress that would pay them early. Soon, an estimated 11,000 to 20,000 veterans – who quickly became known as the Bonus Army – as well as some families, crowded the capital, setting up massive camps in the area, including a makeshift camp on the mud flats of the Anacostia River. An orderly group, the "Bonus Expeditionary Force" as they called themselves, maintained strict military discipline, including bugle calls, chow lines, and liaison officers. They were there for their bonus money and were not there to express anti-American or anti-government sentiments. "Eyes front – not left" was their motto.

On June 15, the bill was passed in the House of Representatives, but it was rejected by the Senate two days later. The veterans were disappointed, but most reacted peacefully and many returned home – though thousands still remained in the capital.

In late July, after Congress had adjourned, the government decided that the veterans should vacate the abandoned buildings they had occupied along Pennsylvania Avenue. However, the veterans refused to leave, and on July 28 violence broke out between veterans and police, resulting in the deaths of two veterans.

At that point, President Herbert C. Hoover called out the Army to intervene. About 600 soldiers – cavalrymen and infantrymen – along with a few tanks advanced to the scene under the command of Chief of Staff of the U.S. Army Douglas MacArthur. MacArthur's forces numbered two generals and several junior officers, including Majors Dwight D. Eisenhower and George S. Patton, Jr. The troops used tear gas, bayonets, sabers, and tanks to push the veterans out of the downtown area, and then, using similar tactics, MacArthur proceeded to clear out the veterans' main camp at Anacostia Flats, which went up in flames.

Though the government claimed that the troops only used minimal force, and alleged that many of the marchers who were routed were radicals and criminals rather than veterans, the public reacted negatively to the use of military force against American citizens, most of whom were veterans. This incident tarnished the Army's public image, and also increased the public's dissatisfaction with President Herbert Hoover, making him seem heartless. Hoover, a good and sensitive man, soon became America's most hated President. His re-election in 1932 seemed unlikely, and his campaign was further weakened by the defection of a group of progressive Republicans to Democratic candidate Franklin D. Roosevelt. Roosevelt's campaign was vigorous and positive. The

NO VETERAN'S BENEFITS FOR AN INJURED HERO

 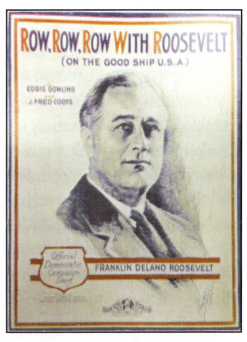

The smiling, confident New York governor, Franklin Delano Roosevelt promised action and a change of direction in the 1932 election. On the right is the cover of a 1933 campaign song. *Library of Congress.*

song "Happy Days Are Here Again" followed him throughout the election. However, happy days did not come immediately for the Bonus Army. The early bonus payments the veterans sought were not approved until 1936, and Willie Sandlin's did not come until many years after his death. [32]

* * *

President Hoover's attempts to combat the growing national financial crisis were largely ineffective. But Sandlin and America's rural poor, though angry and desperate, did not lose faith in their government. In 1932, their patience was rewarded with the election of Franklin D. Roosevelt whose New Deal programs soon had millions of Americans working again. America had a president who truly believed that the federal government had a responsibility

Roosevelt's inaugural address foreshadowed a new course of action for a nation mired in the Great Depression. The president's nationally broadcast statement on March 4, 1933, brought hope and cheer to a disheartened nation. *Library of Congress.*

for the welfare of every citizen. FDR had replaced America's fear with the confidence that the economy would improve. "The whole country is with him," reported Will Rogers in a March 5 newspaper column.[33]

FDR in 1936. Roosevelt's dynamic enthusiasm captured the imagination of voters. In Appalachia, tens of thousands of mountain Republicans became mountain Democrats in an effort to secure work with the Works Progress Administration, the Civilian Conservation Corps, and other New Deal public works programs. *Library of Congress.*

Willie Sandlin in front of the house the built in the 1930s. The house is still standing today.

Photo courtesy of Leona Nichols.

*They shall beat their swords into plowshares
and their spears into pruning hooks.*

Isiah 2:4

CHAPTER SEVEN
SUBSISTENCE FARM LIFE

By the beginning of the Great Depression, Willie Sandlin realized that he would probably not receive any money from the Veterans Administration to compensate him for his war-sustained injuries. So the Sandlins did what tens of thousands of Appalachian families did: "they hunkered down" and "did the best they could with what they had." They became subsistence farmers. Drawing on practices that were more than a century old, subsistence farmers, like the Sandlins, produced almost everything they needed from their farms and nearby fields and forests. They raised cows, hogs, and chickens for meat, which was supplemented by food from vegetable gardens and orchards. The Sandlins did not grow tobacco although someone in Talladega, Kentucky, used Willie's name when selling a tobacco crop. Consequently, newspaper reports stated that "the sergeant had raised and delivered a crop of tobacco to the Lexington market." The story received "wide publicity," and Sandlin was quick to report that he was not "a tobacco grower despite published accounts to the contrary." [1]

The few mainstream reporters who visited Leslie County in the 1920s and 1930s thought everyone was poor. Leslie County had no paved roads. Few homes had electricity or indoor plumbing. But appearances are often deceiving.

SERGEANT SANDLIN

Willie Sandlin and his dog near the front of his house.
Photo courtesy of Leona Nichols.

Belvia's family was wealthy by the standards of that time and place, and they were "land rich." During the 1930s, the Roberts had gifted farm land to Willie and Belvia. "When I was a child, the farm seemed as big as an airport," reflected Willie's daughter Florence. The heart of the farm was a large, stone house which is still standing today. The stone was quarried from the nearby hills by Belvia's brother, who cut and shaped the stones and helped to build the house. Although Willie had little formal education, he was, like many of his contemporaries, a practical genius, and he designed and supervised the construction of his home. Sandlin's home was double-walled with 18 inches between the walls for insulation. A great chimney was a prominent feature of the two-story house. On the lower floor, the chimney had two, back-to-back fireplaces. One warmed the large kitchen and dining room, and the other warmed the downstairs guest

SUBSISTENCE FARM LIFE

room, which was often occupied by visiting family members or school children who were not able to get home after school because of inclement weather or problems with roads or bridges. Willie and Belvia were quick to help children. After their daughter Vorres married and left home, they kept several girls, over the years, who slept upstairs with their unmarried daughters and became informal members of the family while they attended school in Hyden. On the second floor, the design was the same. One fireplace warmed Willie and Belvia's room; the other warmed the bedroom for the girls. "Dad banked the fires at night, no matter how sick he was," said Florence. The only boy, Robert E. Lee Sandlin, had a small bedroom carved out of the girls' bedroom.

Sandlin also designed and implemented an ingenious water system for his home. A sulphur-water spring emerged from the rocks on a hill above the Sandlin home. Willie built a small building around the spring, lined with rocks to filter the sulphur-water before it traveled by an underground pipe to an underground cistern that Willie constructed near his home. From the cistern, underground pipes carried the water into the house to provide water at the kitchen sink, water at the bathroom sink, and water to drive a flush toilet. With hired help, Willie also built a barn, a coal house, a "big, long" chicken house, a corn shed, and a number of other out buildings.

Willie and Belvia each maintained a large garden, one on each side of the barn, and they enjoyed a good-natured competition over their produce, which included "all kinds of vegetables": corn, beans, Irish and sweet potatoes, squash, tomatoes, cabbage, lettuce, kale, and turnip greens, along with green peas and field peas. Willie also maintained a small orchard and was particularly proud of his grapes. Grandma and Grandpa Roberts (Nannie and Pap) had a large orchard on their farm and shared peaches, pears, and apples with their daughter's family. In addition to his vegetable garden, Willie also had large fields of hay and corn. When Florence and "Brother" were little, they were required to hoe corn and each was assigned a long row. On one occasion, Florence was toiling away on her row and looked back to see that little brother Bob was far

SERGEANT SANDLIN

behind and "he was fighting the sweat bees." So, she "went back to help him." Florence and Bob worked in the fields until they entered high school. Often, when they reached the end of their assigned row, which was near the river, they threw down their hoes, climbed the fence, and jumped in the river. Willie and Belvia taught their children to swim at an early age and did not worry "too much" when they were playing in the river.

Willie and Belvia did a great deal of the farm work, but Willie was also working at a WPA job, so "hired hands" worked the corn fields, gathered the hay, and helped with a wide variety of farm chores. The harvested corn was kept in a separate building – the corn shed – and the baled hay was stored in the barn loft. Belvia always fixed the hired hands a big mid-day meal – dinner to the people of Appalachia – often consisting of chicken and dumplings, country ham, green beans, cabbage, kraut, potatoes, tomatoes, hot biscuits and butter, and a dessert. Willie, who was extremely proud of his wife, often bragged that Belvia "could catch a chicken and have dinner on the table in thirty minutes."

Willie's WPA job was a mixed blessing. Although it helped him support a growing family, it was a high-profile job, envied by many Leslie Countians. On one occasion, according to Sandlin family lore, a man who aspired to Willie's job hired a local man to murder the great war hero. True secrets are scarce in small towns, and Willie eventually "got wind" of a rumor about an attempt on his life. As he walked home from Hyden one day, he noticed a man following him. Willie turned and presented a direct question: "Have you been hired to kill me?" The assassin was startled by Willie's non-confrontational, almost casual, tone. His one-word reply was, "Yes."

So Willie said, "Why do you want to kill me?" The would-be killer explained that, like millions of depression-era men, he was broke, out of work, and desperate to support his family. Willie replied, "How would you like a job?"

And so the man who had been hired to kill Willie Sandlin became a member of Leslie County's WPA road crew. Willie's friends passed a message to the man who hired the former assassin: "As you sow, so shall you reap. Stay

Willie as a WPA road supervisor in the 1930s. *Kentucky Department of Libraries and Archives.*

SERGEANT SANDLIN

> *One evening, Prince's loud barking alerted the family to an intruder who was stealing chickens. Willie was away, so* **Belvia, who was a good shot, got Willie's Luger and shot the man in the leg from her son's window on the second floor of the house.** *As it turned out, the chicken thief was one of Willie's hired hands.*

---

away from Willie Sandlin!" [2]

The Sandlin farm contained a number of animals, including two cows and a bull. When the bull was gone for several days, Florence asked where he was and Willie told his little daughter that he had "loaned him out." The Sandlins also had pigs and chickens and Pap kept sheep. The Sandlins did not have goats, ducks, turkeys, or geese. Belvia made Willie a blanket from sheep's wool that is still a treasured family heirloom. Most Appalachian farm families had a dog, and the Sandlins were no exception. "Old Prince" was a good-natured bulldog who provided companionship and security. He went with the children when they brought in the cows and scared the snakes away. Old Prince was an outside guard dog, but he ate in the house with his family at night. The children slipped table scraps to him. "Daddy knew what we were doing, but Mother did not," remembered Florence. In extremely cold weather, Prince slept inside next to the downstairs fireplace.

One evening, Prince's loud barking alerted the family to an intruder who was stealing chickens. Willie was away, so Belvia, who was a good shot, got Willie's Luger and shot the man in the leg from her son's window on the second floor of the house. As it turned out, the chicken thief was one of Willie's hired hands. The next day at work, Willie asked the man why he was limping, and the chicken-thief replied, "Your wife shot me!" Willie had no sympathy for him. "If

SUBSISTENCE FARM LIFE

you had asked her for food, she would have given you more than you asked for," Willie replied. Later, he told his children, "Mother would have given him a chicken if he had asked."

A mountain farm was incomplete without a mule, and Willie did not own one. So, Willie and Belvia gave Florence's older sister Vorres and her husband enough land to build a house and raise a garden in exchange for their mule. The Sandlins also owned a horse named Old Bob. Willie often rode Bob to town rather than walk the half mile into Hyden. After Willie died, his daughter Florence found a Case knife that was Willie's constant companion. "Dad had cut my initials on it," she said, "and he notched it every year 'till I was 16."

Hogs were the most important animals raised by the Sandlins and other depression-era subsistence farmers. In fact, the hog was almost as important to subsistence farmers as the buffalo was to the Indians of the Great Plains. In October, selected hogs were penned and fattened to be butchered in November or December. It was hard, but productive, work that involved the Sandlin family and several other helpers. The helpers were paid in part with tenderloin and other cuts of meat. Some brought pails to catch the blood and made blood pudding. Others took home the feet and the head of the butchered hog. Almost every part of the animal was used by the Sandlins and their thrifty neighbors. Hams, bacon, sausage, salt pork, lard, and soap were just some of the by-products of "hog killing." The meat was preserved and cured in Grandpa Roberts' smokehouse. Lard, rendered from hog fat, was an essential ingredient of Belvia's cooking. Pork barbeque, which would become a regional delicacy before it was commercialized nationally, was not a part of Belvia Sandlin's menus.

Chickens were also a key component of the Sandlin foodways, and they provided a variety of products, too – feathers, eggs, and meat. The long chicken house was very secure and the Sandlins had no problems with foxes or hawks. Belvia's fried chicken was a memorable Sunday meal. Her chicken parts were dredged in flour, seasoned, and then fried in hog fat. Although Belvia cooked with lard, she lived to be almost 97 and never had a cholesterol or a heart

SERGEANT SANDLIN

problem. During the depression, fried chicken was usually eaten during the warm weather, after hens hatched chicks that grew into tender young fryers. Every day, Belvia and her children went to the chicken house and gathered eggs. Normally, they picked up about two baskets full. Belvia used the eggs in her cooking, and she gave away the ones she could not use to less fortunate families. Unlike many subsistence farmers, the Sandlins did not sell or trade eggs for income.

> *Belvia loved to make desserts, and she served a dessert at every meal,* **a family tradition continued by her daughters into the twenty-first century**.

Belvia cooked on a kitchen stove that was heated by both wood and coal. Chopping firewood was a chore for children and adults in the Sandlin family. Uncle Watt kept firewood stacked under the front porch, so that it would be dry and accessible. Children normally brought in the wood and the coal for the stove and the fireplaces. Belvia always fixed a big breakfast that would contain biscuits, sausage gravy, and bacon or sausage. One of her specialties was pancakes, which she served with butter and homemade syrup. Belvia loved to make desserts, and she served a dessert at every meal, a family tradition continued by her daughters into the twenty-first century. In addition to pies and cakes, she made wonderful donuts, covered with cinnamon or powdered sugar, that always brought a smile to her family and her many guests. Another specialty was gingerbread made from molasses. Belvia's daughters all became good cooks by watching their mother cook. They also became proficient at canning.

Another important kitchen appliance was the ice box which resided on the back porch. Belvia had ordered it from a catalog. It was smaller than today's refrigerators, and its primary purpose was to keep milk and butter cool. Other homes in the Hyden area had ice boxes, so there was an ice plant in Hyden that delivered ice to area homes. In the 1930s, when Willie was working each day, his youngest children, Florence and Bob, were responsible for helping to deliver

SUBSISTENCE FARM LIFE

the ice. The ice truck came out Dry Hill Road to the swinging bridge that crossed the river to the property owned by the Sandlins and the Roberts. Normally, the ice was delivered in a large block that fit the ice box, but Willie arranged for the block to be cut in half so his two children could carry it. The half blocks were in two cloth bags with handles, and Florence and Bob carried their bags across the bridge and to their home – a distance of about one city block today. They returned the bags as part of the next ice delivery. Although the Sandlin home did not have electric lights, it did have a telephone, so Belvia was able to call the ice plant and place an order, when necessary.

Belvia canned hundreds of jars of vegetables to supplement the meats she served. Many subsistence farmers preserved potatoes by holing them up in a potato pit. However, the Sandlins had a food cellar that was below their kitchen and Belvia made regular trips downstairs to retrieve canned vegetables, fruits, "shucky beans," and dried apples. Irish and sweet potatoes were stored in the food cellar in layers of straw. Throughout the depression, the Sandlins gave food to friends and neighbors who were "down on their luck." The Sandlins enjoyed corn, but they grew large fields of corn primarily to provide feed for the livestock. The Sandlins did not raise tobacco, wheat, or oats.

Willie's father-in-law, William Roberts (Pap to his grandchildren), was truly a community leader. He owned the phone company; he owned and operated a small country store in a separate building that stood near his barn; and he was an unofficial banker, loaning thousands of (never re-paid) dollars to help his neighbors and friends survive the depression. He also had a large farm and was an enthusiastic farmer. On Saturdays, during the warm days of summer and fall, William operated a mill to help his neighbors, who brought corn which was ground into meal and poured into brown burlap sacks which William provided. William knew his proud neighbors well, so he did not operate a "free" mill. He charged fifty cents per customer and assigned the responsibility of collecting the fees to his granddaughter, Florence, a little blonde beauty who bore some resemblance to Shirley Temple.

BELVIA'S PARENTS

Parents:
William Roberts (February 25, 1862 - December 7, 1941)
Sally Ann Roberts (1864 - 1955)
Married in 1885

Sally Ann Roberts had two sons named David and James with Thomas Hensley before her marriage to William.

William Roberts had a child before his marriage to Sally Ann with a woman named Betsy Asher. This child, James Roberts (June 4, 1881 - September 18, 1952), was later adopted by William and Sally. According to family legend, Betsy Asher came by William's house on a horse and dropped the 4-year-old off over the fence saying to Sally Ann, "This is your husband's child and you need to raise him." William denied him to the day he died.

Their children:
- Sophia Roberts Cook (August 12, 1887 - April 1, 1986)
- Eva Roberts Nance (February 24, 1890 - December 23, 1970)
- Virgil Roberts (April 27, 1891 - October 18, 1923)
- Cash Roberts (born ca. 1893)
- Walt H. Roberts (May 10, 1895 - June 10, 1962)
- Zora Roberts (April, 1899 - May 3, 1970)
- Belvia Roberts Sandlin (June 16, 1902 - February 5, 1999)
- Ottis Roberts (December 31, 1904 - October 18, 1965)
- Golden Roberts (August 25, 1906 - February 19, 1984)

This chart is based on genealogical research.

SUBSISTENCE FARM LIFE

Belvia's parents, William and Sally Ann Roberts. *Photo courtesy of James Roberts.*

Milling corn was a family affair. While William ground his neighbors' corn into meal, his wife, Sally Ann (Nannie to her grandchildren) provided a noon meal for the families that came to benefit from Pap's mill. She and her grandchildren set up tables and chairs in the shade of large trees and provided a bountiful meal for their neighbors. When Florence was not collecting milling fees, she was "shooing away the flies" from her Nannie's tables.

To reward her hard work, Pap paid Florence fifty cents. Florence immediately took her half dollar to Pap's store and purchased fifty cents' worth of candy from Nannie who was minding the store while Pap operated the mill. Florence proceeded to share her candy with the little children who were playing near the river – waiting for their parents to signal the time to return home.

During the decade of the depression, Willie and Belvia both worked extremely hard to make a good life and a good home for their children. Willie had regular diversions away from home and work. The responsibilities of gardening, cooking, cleaning, and taking care of her home and children diminished Belvia's mobility and lessened the diversions available to her. Her

SERGEANT SANDLIN

Mountain people bring garden produce to town to peddle and trade for other necessities. Jackson, Breathitt County, Kentucky, September 1940. *Farm Security Administration photos, Library of Congress.*

duties were dull when contrasted with Willie's more exciting opportunities to hunt, fish, and enjoy the beauty and solitude of the out-of-doors world. However, neither Willie nor Belvia questioned nor sought to alter the roles they played. The danger inherent in Willie's life and the drudgeries that Belvia experienced were gracefully accepted as part of the unspoken survival pact that intensified the love, appreciation, and mutual respect of their marriage.

Laundry day was one of Belvia's greatest burdens. Because the Sandlin's home lacked electricity, Belvia followed the laundry-day practices of her pioneer ancestors. It took all day for Belvia to wash the family's clothes and other washable items, so she had to get a day ahead in her cooking. On pretty days, the laundry was done outside with a scrub board and two galvanized tubs. The clothes were soaked in cold water, then they were removed and scrubbed, and finally the clothes went to the second tub of hot water along with soap. For the next three or four hours, the hot water was stirred with a long-handled wooden paddle to keep the soap in the clothes. Finally, they were removed, soaked again in cold water, and hung up to dry.

Another responsibility that fell heavily on Belvia was family health care. Although she had doctors and nurses from the Frontier Nursing Service to assist with major problems, the daily health care of the children was Belvia's responsibility. In September 1925, for example, she was concerned because Cora had been very sick "with the same trouble Vorres had – tonsils." The next month, little Cora was dead. In 1932, she and Willie were suffering from a cold he had contracted while in Louisville. That fall she reported that the entire family had had colds and that Vorres and Leona had been very sick for a week. The next month, she reported that everyone in the family was well except her and the baby, Robert E. Lee Sandlin, who was cutting teeth and soon to celebrate his first birthday. [3] Like many of her contemporaries, her health care system was a combination of faith, common sense, and home remedies.

The Sandlins at Play

Unlike people of other times and places, subsistence farmers did not lead lives that were clearly divided into categories of work and play. In fact, those areas often overlapped and became synonymous. For example, when Willie Sandlin hunted or fished, he was both at work and at play. Willie loved the natural world, and he was a crack shot and an enthusiastic hunter and fisherman. When he hunted, it was normal for him to bring home rabbits, squirrels, or deer. His little daughter Florence would cry if he killed an animal and refuse to eat it when it was prepared and cooked. When Willie went fishing, he would clean the fish and Belvia would fry them. Willie's older girls did not eat fish for fear of swallowing a bone, but everyone else in the family would laugh and say, "That's just more for the rest of us."

SERGEANT SANDLIN

When Willie's son was old enough, his father taught him to hunt. Florence wanted to go, too, but Willie teasingly told her that she could never hunt with the men of the family because she was too loud and "talked too much." Later, when Bob was a little older, Willie gave his son a sawed-off shotgun that Willie had received as a gift. Florence asked to shoot it after Bob learned to use the gun. Finally, Willie relented and propped the gun on a fence and Florence took her first shot. The shotgun recoil knocked the thirteen-year-old girl to the ground, and Florence never asked to shoot the shotgun again.

In the 1930s and 1940s, Willie continued to be actively involved as a loving parent.
Florence Muncy Collection.

In warm weather, Willie and Belvia hosted square dances for their children and other young people from the community. The Sandlins moved all the downstairs furniture outside to the front and back porches and opened the house for the dancers. Music was provided by local adults, including Belvia's mother, Sally Ann, a wonderful fiddler. Willie often said Sally Ann "could make her fiddle talk." The Sandlin children loved to see Willie and Belvia dance," remembered Leona.

In the winter, when the river froze, Willie built a big bonfire near the bank, and the family went ice skating together. Willie was a graceful skater and he could "dance on his skates." When Bob was little and learning to skate, his parents tied a rope around his waist and inserted a pillow "on his back side" to

SUBSISTENCE FARM LIFE

cushion his falls.

Although much of their entertainment was family oriented, Willie loved to get out "with the boys" occasionally. He and other men went coon hunting at night. Sometimes, Willie went to town to play cards at the store with the mayor and other business leaders. It was harmless fun, but sometimes he returned home late and that displeased his wife. Willie would laugh and tell his children that when he got home he would throw his hat into the bedroom. If Belvia "threw it back," he knew he was in trouble. Willie was also an active member of the Masonic lodge in Hyden, Number 664, where he was initiated on July 11, 1928. He played a leadership role after becoming a member, first serving as a Deacon. Later he served as Junior Warden, Steward, Tyler, and Trustee. While serving as Trustee, Willie helped to acquire the building that housed the Masonic Temple he served faithfully and well for many years.

Belvia had her own version of today's "girls' night out" entertainments. Willie had made her a fancy quilting frame that hung by ropes and hooks from the ceiling when it was not in use. When Belvia hosted a quilting party, she invited four or five local women and they would work together – usually meeting at least three times – to complete a quilt. Then they would go through the same process again with another member of their group. Each woman would supply her own material and pattern. The finished quilt, with its thousands of small hand stitches, was always beautiful. In today's language, the quilting bees provided Belvia and her friends with an opportunity to reaffirm their sisterhood. Belvia always prepared food and desserts for the quilters.

Before the quilt was finished, all the young, unmarried girls gathered around the quilt for a fascinating Leslie County tradition – the "cat shaking." The house cat was captured and placed in the center of the quilt while the quilters grabbed the four sides and tossed the bewildered cat up and down. When the cat managed to escape, according to local custom, the young girl standing closest to the escaping cat was going to be the next bride in the community. Belvia and her neighbors had great fun with this activity. [4]

Other Superstitions and Folk Beliefs

While the "cat shaking" was probably a practice unique to Leslie County, Willie Sandlin and his neighbors had a number of superstitions and beliefs that emerged from the broader Appalachian culture. Some of the beliefs were based on practice and experience and were more factually grounded than superstitions. For example, using the moon's guidance for planting crops and killing hogs was based upon a passage from Genesis 1:14. Sandlin and his neighbors would never plant corn during the first three days of May, because the crop would be barren, nor would they plant in the rise of the moon. Root crops, such as potatoes, were planted when the moon was new. If they were planted during the "old phase" of the moon, the potatoes, according to local belief, would root deep into the ground and be hard to dig; however, they must be dug during the "old phase" of the moon. Belvia and the women of Leslie County used the moon's guidance in making soap. If they made it during the wrong moon sign, it would not harden. Hogs had to be killed during the old moon on dark nights to keep the meat from being tough and bloated.

> *The women of Leslie County **used the moon's guidance in making soap**. If they made it during the wrong moon sign, it would not harden. Hogs had to be killed during the old moon on dark nights to keep the meat from being tough and bloated.*

The moon and other natural signs foretold the weather for Leslie Countians. If tree leaves turned upside down when the wind blew, then bad weather would arrive soon. A pale moon indicated rain. If there was a ring around the moon, the number of stars inside the ring meant that many more fair days. Dew on the grass at night or in the early morning was a sign of fair weather.

Birds and animals helped to predict the weather, too. Wild geese flying south meant bad weather would arrive within three days. Owls hooting at night or roosters crowing at night were other omens of approaching bad weather. If chickens sought shelter in a morning rain, the rain would stop soon, but if they tightened their feathers and remained outside, the rain would continue all day. Birds perching more than usual indicated approaching storms. A whippoorwill calling at night meant no rain that night.

If a muskrat built a low house of reeds and mud, the approaching winter would be mild, but if he burrowed beneath the ground, then Leslie Countians expected a severe winter. Frogs croaking signified approaching storms. If chimney smoke did not rise, stormy weather was coming. Wooly worms helped to predict weather, too. If its coat was completely black, it meant a bad winter. If only partly black, it meant the black end of the worm signified the beginning (or the end) of winter would be the hardest part.

A lot of snow meant good crops the following year. The number of fogs in August foretold the number of winter snows. If it thundered in February, it would frost on that same day in May. A new moon standing on end would pour out water, so within three days it would rain or snow. The moon on its back was a sign of dry weather. Lots of insect activity meant a storm was approaching. Counting the number of chirps a cricket made in 14 seconds and adding 40 gave the temperature.

Many manners and social customs derived from older practices. For example, the handshake was to demonstrate the absence of a concealed weapon. Covering one's mouth while yawning became good manners, but originally it was done to keep evil spirits from entering the body.

Folkways and superstitions actively influenced the lives of the Sandlins and their neighbors. [5]

* * *

During the 1930s, Belvia sometimes took her children to Hazard for an outing. They rode a local bus – the Black Brothers Bus – that traveled to Hazard and back regularly and stopped for passengers along the way. In the mid-1930s, when her youngest daughter was six or seven years old, Belvia and Florence traveled to Hazard together because Florence wanted to see a movie starring her idol, Shirley Temple. They traveled with Dr. John Kooser and his wife. Dr. Kooser was the Medical Director for the Frontier Nursing Service in Hyden. He and his wife lived in a big house in Hyden, but they traveled to Hazard frequently to enjoy the "big-city amenities" – more than one grocery store and a movie theatre. Dr. Kooser and Belvia went grocery shopping, while his wife and little Florence went to a movie. After they returned from the movie, Belvia held her little daughter and said, "I'll take you to the 10¢ store and buy you anything you want, but you have to do one thing for me."

"What's that, Mommy?"

"I want you to say that you're my baby girl and not Daddy's," said Belvia.

"I can't say that, Mommy. I'm Daddy's baby girl!"

Good Parents at Church and School

Religious practices in Hyden and other small, isolated eastern Kentucky communities reflected the practices of the independent pioneers who settled eastern Kentucky in the 1700s and 1800s. These hardy pioneers had rejected the ways of the New England townsmen and the coastal planters, and they had rejected their religions, also. The isolated settlers beyond the Blue Ridge developed a unique culture that was not a part of the colonial mainstream, nor was it patterned after European models. It was "American" long before the United States of America formally existed.

Early settlers in eastern Kentucky developed institutions that were suited to their needs. They were not formal people, and they did not want a formal religion. They were direct people who worshipped in churches that allowed them to pray directly, earnestly, and emotionally to their God. Many of the Scotch-Irish settlers were Presbyterians and many of the English settlers were Methodists. Along with the Baptists, they were the main churches in Hyden during the 1930s and 1940s. Willie and Belvia raised their children in the Presbyterian Church in

GREETINGS:

THIS CERTIFICATE is to recognize *Belma Sandlin*
as the NO. 2 lady in the South American Missionary Class. She
has earned this place because of her diligence in attendance
in the Sunday School and other services of the Church, in reading God's Word and in encouraging others to attend.
May the Lord continue to bless and use you for His glory.

SOUTH AMERICAN MISSIONARY CLASS

Signed

Roma C. Clark
Teacher

Nellie Duddingston
President

Florence Muncy Collection.

Hyden, the same church Belvia's parents attended all their lives. Belvia's father, William Roberts, was a very religious man and read his Bible daily. In the spring of 1932, Belvia began a Sunday School class in her home attended by 22 to 37 adults. That fall, she reported that her class was "coming along fine" and asked Cora Wilson Stewart to send books or pictures to support her efforts to have a Christmas party for the Sunday School students. "I do not think the pictures and books I have to send would be very suitable for Christmas," Mrs. Stewart replied, "but I shall be glad to send them for your class some time soon. None of us have anything much to give for Christmas this year." [6]

Because Willie suffered from a lack of education as a child, he was determined that his children would receive an education. "Mother came to school activities during the day because Dad was working," said Leona. Sometimes Willie and Belvia walked to school at night to see basketball games and watch their daughter, Florence, who was a high school cheerleader. At other times, one of them would walk to the gymnasium and walk their daughter home after the games.

Clothing for Willie's Family

"Mother never wore a pair of pants in her life," said one of her daughters. In the 1930s and 1940s, the Sandlin girls did not wear pants to school. They wore dresses or skirts with knee socks. However, once when Florence's class made a trip to Cumberland Falls, Belvia told her to put on a pair of brother Bob's jeans, because she was going to do a lot of hiking. "I had to roll the legs up," remembered Florence. She also wore pants when she did farm work. Once, when she had on a pair of jeans, she and Bob were shelling corn for the horses when a mouse ran up her pants leg. Florence began screaming and the poor little mouse got trapped around her knee. Bob rushed to the rescue and hit his sister's leg and killed the mouse. It was a frightening event for Florence and the mouse, and Bob had blood all over his jeans. When her children reached school age, Belvia purchased most of their clothes from stores in Hazard, but she also shopped from several mail order catalogs.

After Willie built the stone house, Belvia bought a great deal of their furniture from mail-order catalogs, [7] but she still purchased a number of daily items and household necessities from pack peddlers who came around once a month with combs, pins, needles, thimbles, hairpins, lace, socks, ribbons, and many other items. The pack peddlers finally became obsolete in the late 1930s and early 1940s as transportation improved in Leslie County. The last of the county's peddlers "was seen many times walking between Wooten and Hazard around 1942." [8]

Willie Sandlin's life as a subsistence farmer offers insight to his character. He was a man who valued work – a man who found honor in work and, through his own example, he taught his children to work. Willie Sandlin had seen the horrors of war and there were days when he suffered from his memories and experiences. Certainly there were days when it was hard for him to be a cheerful father and loving husband, but Sandlin truly loved his home and family.

SUBSISTENCE FARM LIFE

In many ways, Willie Sandlin was the real-life embodiment of John Walton, one of the great fathers of American fiction. They were both rural men, loving husbands and fathers, and veterans of the Great War. In Earl Hamner, Jr.'s classic, *The Homecoming*, Clay-Boy (later to be John-Boy Walton) described his father as

> *. . . a hard man to measure up to. Like all the Spencer (Walton) men he was a crack shot, a good provider for his family, an honest "look-em-in-the-eye" man, an enthusiastic drinker, a prodigious dancer, a fixer of things, a builder, a singer of note, a teller of bawdy stories, a kissing, hugging, loving man whose laughter would shake the house, and who was not ashamed to cry. He seemed to his son an outsized man, bigger than life.* [9]

Except for the enthusiastic drinking, that was Willie Sandlin, too.

"When I turned 21," remembered his daughter Leona, "Daddy came to the Hyden Citizens Bank where I worked and walked me to the court house so I could register to vote. Daddy was proud, honest and trustworthy. Everyone liked and respected him. I never heard an ill word spoken about him. I could not have had better parents or a better childhood."

General landscape near Hyden, Kentucky, showing mountain cabins, sheds and cornfields, August 1940. *Farm Security Administration photos, Library of Congress.*

Willie expected his children to work on the farm. "Whenever he plowed the cornfield," remembered his daughter Leona, "Nancy, Vorres, and I would follow after him and push the loose soil around the stalks. He would have us hoe in the garden. He could always pick out the row I hoed and said mine was best."

Barely breaking the flow of light,
you stood at the edge of the woods,
a shadow man, finding it hard to leave the place.

"New Ghost"
Edwina Pendarvis

CHAPTER EIGHT
HYDEN

When Willie and Belvia were raising their family on Owl's Nest Creek, the town of Hyden, only about one-half mile away, played an important role in their lives. Hyden was a small town – less than one thousand residents – situated in the valley of the Middle Fork of the Kentucky River at the mouth of Rockhouse Creek, a small stream that emptied into the Middle Fork. It was surrounded by mountains. In the 1930s, the hills were dotted with beech, oak, maple, hemlock, poplar, ash, and walnut trees. The land around Hyden was not well-suited to agriculture, but Willie Sandlin's bottom-lands farm was an exception.

Hyden is the county seat of Leslie County, Kentucky's 117th county. It lies on the Cumberland Plateau, bordered by Harlan County on the south, Perry County on the east, and Bell and Clay Counties on its western borders. Located in the eastern part of the Daniel Boone National Forest, Leslie County is approximately 16 miles wide and 28 miles long. The County's 412 square miles are heavily forested. Parts of Leslie County are more than 2500 feet above sea level. By the early twentieth century, the small population was divided into 22 organized communities. [1]

Above: Logging is one of the few sources of income to mountaineers. This cabin with the cornfield above it is near Hyden, Kentucky, September 1940. Below-left: Mountain cabin, general store, and gas station along highway near Hyden, Kentucky, August 1940. Below-right: Homes with gardens, patches of tobacco and corn in mountain section near Hyden, Kentucky, September 1940. *Farm Security Administration photos, Library of Congress.*

HYDEN

General landscape near Hyden, Kentucky, showing mountain cabins, sheds, and cornfields, August 1940. *Farm Security Administration photos, Library of Congress.*

Leslie County had been created in 1878 and named for Kentucky Governor Preston H. Leslie. Hyden, the county seat, was named after John Hyden, a senator and former judge of Perry County. By 1900, a rough plank courthouse that had been built in 1888 had been replaced by a new two-story brick building built in 1897, which was still standing in the 1930s. The main floor included the following offices: Sheriff, County Superintendent, County Court Clerk, Circuit Court Clerk, and County Judge. The Court Room covered the entire second floor and could accommodate more than 100 people. The county jail, a two-story stone structure located at the back of the courthouse, contained offices on the first floor and cages and cells on the second floor. The floors were concrete. In the 1930s, Hyden had no "lighting system nor water system in the town." In

SERGEANT SANDLIN

1921, Leslie County paid $20,000 for 1.7 miles of twenty-foot highway as part of a projected state highway connecting London with Hazard, via Manchester and Hyden. It was the first paved road in the county. [2] A state highway was completed to Hyden in 1931. US 80 crossed the Middle Fork River one-half mile south of Hyden, the only state road completed in the county.

Transportation services to and from Hyden included a local bus that provided 25-mile round-trip service from Hyden to Hazard. The bus left Hyden at 8:30 am and later at 1:00 pm and 5:00 pm and made connections with trains and buses leaving Hazard for Lexington. Willie Sandlin and his family often travelled to Hazard by bus.

In the 1930s, the old grade school building burned and grade school classes and high school classes were both conducted in the high school building which was not large enough to adequately accommodate all the students. A new stone building with 18 rooms and a large auditorium was constructed by the WPA and the county in the 1930s. This building housed the only school in Hyden. The town also contained dormitories for boys and girls who lived "out in the county" and

In the 1930s and 1940s, many people still walked to town for supplies. *Farm Security Administration photos, Library of Congress.*

could not have attended school without a place to live near the school. The dormitories were provided and supported by the Baptist Church and the Presbyterian Church. In the 1930s, there were four churches: the Baptist Church was located in Hyden; the Presbyterian Church at the "Northern End;" the Christian Church at the south central part of the city; and the "Evangelical"

Rural mailman going up the creek bed toward Morris Fork near Jackson, Kentucky, August 1940. *Farm Security Administration photos, Library of Congress.*

Mountain horse with sack of beans on his saddle, Jackson, Kentucky, August 1940. *Farm Security Administration photos, Library of Congress.*

was in the western part.

The churches held a yearly conference the last week of June for the young people between the ages of 12 and 20. They either brought their lunch or paid two dollars per week for meals. Ten instructors worked with all four churches. All the student "work and play" was supervised. At the end of one conference, a young man wrote, "We have blazed a new trail and hope to keep it going."

The Presbyterian Church was established in Hyden in 1894. Two years later, the church dedicated the Academy Building for "both religious and educational work." At that time, the Presbyterians also created a two-story white frame building for a girl's dormitory. It was named the Giddings Home to honor Anna Giddings who died of typhoid fever while she was teaching in Hyden. Both the Academy Building and the Giddings Home were later destroyed by fire. The Presbyterian church did not rebuild the Academy Building, because Leslie County built a new high school building with WPA assistance. However, the Presbyterians did build two new dormitories. The boys' and girls' dormitories were operated by "Christian workers" and accommodated boys and girls "from out in the county who could not go to school without this opportunity." Miss Mabel Byers and her sister Lila had served in Hyden "in ardent Christian service" for more than twenty years when they were placed in charge of the girls' dormitory.

The Presbyterian Church in Hyden was constructed of rough gray stone. It was considered to be "very artistic and modernistic," with pews that had been donated by the Old Central Presbyterian Church of New York City. The church building had a "private lighting plant" that was supported, in part, by gifts from Miss Ruth Houston, a "very capable young woman from Pennsylvania." Ruth was a millionaire's daughter who had devoted her life to Christian work in Hyden. Willie and Belvia were very impressed with Ruth Houston and named their fourth child after her; Nancy Ruth Sandlin was born December 28, 1926. Miss Houston built a modern home in Hyden "equipped with bath, sleeping porch, electric lights, and running water." Several of the dormitory girls stayed with her every year and enjoyed the advantages of Miss Houston's modern home.

The old manse was used for the boys' dormitory. One of the most beautiful homes in Leslie County, it was designed by Mrs. McKee, the wife of the Presbyterian minister who served in the 1920s and 1930s. Mrs. McKee, a medical doctor and a graduate of Johns Hopkins, met and married her husband when they were both serving as missionaries in China. After they returned to the States, they continued their life of service in Hyden. Mrs. McKee had an office in her home that included a closet for medical supplies and a waiting room. The McKees left Hyden in the 1930s, and Mrs. McKee died of a brain tumor shortly after they departed Leslie County.

Although the Presbyterian Church did not own or control the new school that was built and managed by the County Board of Education, the church continued to play an important role by supplying teachers and by housing students in the church-maintained dormitories.

The county also owned a large yellow school bus that traveled ten miles to the east of Hyden and twelve miles to the west. This bus serviced high school students who lived within three miles of the highway and brought them to and from school each day.

In addition to the schools, the dormitories, and the churches, Hyden contained one bank, the Hyden Citizens Bank, which had employed Willie's daughter Vorres after she graduated from high school, and one hotel, the Johnson Hotel, owned and operated by Drucilla Lewis on the "European Plan," rooms for fifty cents per day and meals for thirty-five cents. The Johnson Hotel contained eighteen guest rooms, a lobby, and a large dining room. The lobby was furnished with an old fashioned davenport and two large writing tables and chairs; the dining room contained four tables; each one seated eight people. The kitchen was equipped with a coal stove, a "water table," and a sink. The hotel was steam heated and lit by oil lamps. There was no bath.

Campbell's corner drug store, owned and operated by Ruford and "Pet" Campbell, was a center of commerce and communication. It was the only drug

Left: Mountain woman churning butter on the steps of front porch of her home, up Burton's Fork off Middle Fork of the Kentucky River, Breathitt County, Kentucky, September 1940.

Below: Mountain family on porch of their home made of hand hewn logs, up South Fork of Kentucky River, Breathitt County, Kentucky" Sept 1940.

Farm Security Administration photos, Library of Congress.

store between Hazard and Manchester. Although it did not fill prescriptions, it did provide fountain service and also served as the bus station. The manager's wife sold bus tickets from a counter in the store. Although the town was ostensibly dry, WPA interviewers reported that Hyden also contained two "whiskey and lunch rooms" owned by Sarah Arnold and Maggie Sizemore. The town contained four general stores, with stock averaging about $5000 for each store and one wholesale store. Often, when people rode mules or horses to town, they left them in William Roberts' stable and walked the last half-mile into town, where they shopped and conducted personal business. A dentist, Dr. G. G. Maggard, spent part of his time working in Hyden and the remainder of his time in Clay County, but Dr. Maggard was always in Hyden when Circuit Court met in March, August, and November.

Leslie County's only newspaper, *Thousandsticks*, was located in a small building behind the Citizens Bank in Hyden. The paper was owned and operated by J. M. Muncy, who established the paper in 1898. The paper was a weekly paper – four-page paper each Thursday – and was named for the highest hill in the county. The paper enjoyed a circulation of about 800 subscribers and it was distributed to many parts of the United States and to several foreign nations. Muncy also used his newspaper equipment to do "job printing," advertising, and election ballots. The paper was unique in that it kept "the natural dialect of the mountain people." *Thousandsticks* descended from *The Leslie Banner*, which was edited and managed by Belvia's father, William B. Roberts. The *Banner* professed to be a "Republican paper" that tried to give a "square deal" to all. This "good, clean, local paper" supported good roads, good schools, more and better churches, and "anything that will advance Leslie County educationally and morally." [3]

Hyden contained one garage with a mechanic and two filling stations. Although there were no tourist camps in Hyden, there was a resort one-half mile out of Hyden on US 80 where the highway bridge crossed the Middle Fork River. The "Whirl Pool Inn" was located on the bank of the Middle Fork River and

"Mountaineer riding on muleback up a creek bed to his farm. Breathitt County, Kentucky" Sept 1940

"Carrying home groceries and supplies across the swinging bridge, Breathitt County, Jackson, Kentucky" Sept 1940

Hyden farmstead, Oct. 1940. Wolcott FSA photograph. *Library of Congress.*

provided facilities for visitors to dine and dance. The Whirl Pool Inn was surrounded by rhododendron, mountain laurel, pines, and rocks and was suitable for picnics. It was open every day and night except Sunday night. There was no movie theatre in Hyden.[4] The nearest one was in Hazard, twenty-five miles away.

When Willie Sandlin returned to Hyden after World War I, the small, isolated community remained tied to nineteenth century Appalachian life and culture. A little more than a decade later, during the depression, Hyden and its residents began to adopt a lifestyle that was more consistent with the twentieth century. Hyden was not seeking modernity during the 1930s as much as modernity gradually arrived in Hyden.

For example, in 1933 the University of Kentucky established "listening centers" in isolated parts of eastern Kentucky where few radios existed. Although Willie and Belvia had a battery-powered radio, in 1933 there were still homes and whole communities where people opined, "You can't tell me that you are pullin' music out of the air." Because electric current was not available in many places in the mountains, battery sets were essential for radio service.

On their third installation trip, July 22, 1933, the university radio men installed and tested a battery set at Wooten Center in Leslie County. They then insulated the aerial and put in a working set for Hyden Community Center, where there were four non-working battery sets. These battery sets were later "reconditioned" and installed in Leslie County sites at Thousandsticks, Dry Hill, Stinnett, and Beech Fork.

Of these listening centers, University of Kentucky president Frank L. McVey declared that

> *Through the installation of radio receiving sets in these remote districts, the University of Kentucky hopes to bring to the people some of the wonders of the great invention. Through the radio the University hopes to furnish information and enlightenment; perhaps to inspire the listeners to better methods in farming, forestry, and home-making; to bring enjoyment into the centers and homes; and to give to the mountain people a sense of being in communication with their state, their nation, and their world.* [5]

*Now a promise made is a debt unpaid
and the trail has its own stern code.*
  "The Cremation of Sam McGee"
  Robert W. Service

CHAPTER NINE
STILL TRYING FOR FINANCIAL ASSISTANCE IN THE 1930s

Aware of Sandlin's financial difficulties, Senator Hiram Brock, who represented Leslie County in the state legislature, continued his efforts to get funds from the state government to purchase a farm for Sandlin. Senator Brock had been inspired by the American Legion's efforts to raise money to provide a home for Sandlin and his family so they could "live with the common comfort of life." During the 1920s, the VFW had established a "Hero Fund" and called upon "all patriotic citizens," along with members of the Veterans of Foreign Wars and "others throughout the country to mail in their contributions to the VFW, McClelland Building, Lexington, Kentucky." VFW leaders said there would have been no need to raise funds to buy a home for the Sandlins if Willie had been willing to "sell his birthright for a mess of pottage." According to VFW leaders, a "celebrated moving picture concern" had offered Willie $500 a week to re-enact his heroic deeds, but "Sandlin refused to capitalize on his war records" and refused "other offers to profit from his patriotism." Through the "Hero Fund," the VFW still sought to raise $10,000 for the purpose of "buying a farm and home" for war-hero Willie Sandlin. [1] However, a decade of failures along with the financial despair of the depression combined to make this project nothing more than wishful thinking. The 1930 census listed Sandlin as a farmer with property valued at $500.

While the Sandlins probably did not expect a $10,000 windfall during the depression, they still hoped to receive the money that had already been gifted to the Hero Fund. In 1927, the Hero Fund totaled $1300, and five years later not a single dollar had been turned over to Willie Sandlin, the intended recipient. "A bunch of the VFWs in Louisville have the money," wrote Sandlin's wife in June 1932, and "it seems as if they do not want to turn the money over." Willie planned to make a trip to Louisville in July to once again claim money that was rightfully his. Friend and confidante Cora Wilson Stewart advised the Sandlins not to settle and compromise. "Did Sergeant take my letter with him to Louisville and show it them?" she asked Belvia. "I wrote him one about this fund and

Sandlin never received the money that his fellow Kentuckians donated to him through the statewide Hero Fund. *Florence Muncy Collection.*

thought that it might be a good thing for him to produce when he asked for his money. He never answered the letter, so I do not know whether it helped or not." A month later, Belvia reported that Willie's trip to Louisville had been unsuccessful. "They lost the money in a Bank Break [crash]," she explained to Mrs. Stewart. Still Belvia believed that the Bank would pay back some of the

STILL TRYING FOR FINANCIAL ASSISTANCE IN THE 1930s

money on a share [pro rata] basis. The sum of $750 was now worth about $130. "It looks as if we have about lost the money." Belvia reported that a new Department Commander had promised "to try to striating [sic] up the matter some way by the last of this month." [2]

Mrs. Stewart was distressed by this injustice and advised Sergeant Sandlin not to accept the $130 and let Mrs. Stewart and other friends "fight it out with them until the $1300 – the full amount contributed by his friends – is produced. He may be inclined to be easy with those who handled the funds, but believe me I am not." Mrs. Stewart and others "went down in their pockets" and contributed to the Hero Fund and VFW representatives "had no right to hold it up until the depression came and it was lost." The VFW "was liable for it" Mrs. Stewart concluded. [3]

That fall, Belvia wrote that nothing had been "done yet," but a lawyer in Hyden talked with Willie and recommended that J. M. Robinson, a Louisville attorney, "bring a suit" against the VFW. Willie had agreed to this course of action and he and Belvia promised to keep Mrs. Stewart informed of any progress. [4]

Mrs. Stewart was pleased and complimented Belvia for telling her "just what I want to know." Mrs. Stewart enthusiastically encouraged the Sandlins to go forward with legal action. "I certainly think that something should be done to make them hand over the whole amount that Sergeant Sandlin's friends gave for that farm, and I should be glad to get hold of some of the other contributors and make a big stir about it so they will feel that they must produce this money." Stewart reminded Belvia that it was not the contributors' fault that the money had been "squandered or lost in a bank." Again, Stewart advised the Sandlins against compromising for a lesser amount, because she felt that the contributors and an attorney "will get that money for him yet." [5]

In response to various pressures, Herman H. Fox, a recently appointed VFW representative, made the following report on the status of the Sandlin Fund as of October 22, 1932:

120 shares Corporate Trust shares	$753.50
Cash on hand in Liberty Insurance Bank	222.96
Due from Union Central Bank	487.73
	1,464.19

The shares of stock are in the hands of the Quartermaster, in a safety deposit box at Liberty Insurance Bank. $9.38 was added to the fund recently. The Union Central Bank, "now defunct," is about ready to declare another dividend.

This fund for settlement has been turned over to Chaplain Joseph B. Head, Judge Advocate Nathaniel E. Whitney, and myself and I will be more than glad to have this matter settled once and for all.

Fox also reported that he wanted to straighten the matter out earlier, but Comrade Eversole had an idea that Robert E. Lee Murphy "would fight this, why I still do not know." [6]

Responding to a copy of Fox's letter, which had been hand-copied by Belvia Sandlin, Mrs. Stewart, the voice of the donors, observed that Fox's letter clarified the amount of money that belongs to Sergeant Sandlin, "every dollar of which they must pay him. It is not his fault nor the fault of his friends who gave money if some officials in the Kentucky Department of the Veterans of Foreign Wars invested it unwisely and lost it instead of turning it over to him. Their organization must pay it now. It would be unfair to those friends who gave it if Sergeant accepted anything less than the full amount." Mrs. Stewart was adamant in her feelings that every dollar gifted to Sandlin should be provided to him for the purchase of a farm. [7]

Lawsuit

By the fall of 1932, Willie Sandlin had fathered five children, and Belvia was pregnant with their sixth child, Robert E. Lee Sandlin, who was born

STILL TRYING FOR FINANCIAL ASSISTANCE IN THE 1930s

November 2, 1932. Little Cora had died on October 2, 1925, so Willie had a wife, four children, and another on the way. He desperately needed the money the VFW had collected on his behalf, so Sandlin, with Robert E. Lee Murphy acting pro bono as his attorney, demanded that the VFW release the monies that had been donated to him by the general public.

The VFW responded in a letter dated October 22, 1932. On behalf of the VFW, Mr. Herman H. Fox, Commander of the Kentucky Department of the VFW, acknowledged that the VFW owed Sandlin $1,464.19. Fox further acknowledged that rather than giving the money directly to Sandlin, the VFW had purchased 120 shares of stock, which represented about 50% of Sandlin's money. While Fox argued that the VFW was acting in good faith and attempting to grow Sandlin's money, Sandlin family members later disputed this claim and blamed Robert E. Lee Murphy for the loss of funds. [8]

In 1932, the VFW valued and apparently paid $753.50 for 120 shares of stock. In addition, the VFW had $222.96 (of Sandlin's money) in the Liberty Insurance Bank, and $487.73 on deposit at the Union Central Bank. Fox offered the 120 shares to settle the dispute but Sandlin filed a lawsuit against the VFW in 1933 and refused to settle for stock that was worthless or severely devalued as a result of the stock market crash, the bank closings, and the weakened economy of the Great Depression. [9]

Two years passed, and Sandlin filed an amended petition, "Plaintiffs Reply to the Responses of Michael B. Gilligan, George Freeman, and John Sweikel" on June 3, 1935. Apparently these three VFW officials had replaced Mr. Fox and several others whose terms of office had expired. This document stated that a court ruling had been filed against these men asking them to comply with a court order or be held in contempt and ordered to jail until they complied. The court had ordered the three officers to turn over to Sandlin, "all or any properties or moneys in possession of defendant, except the sum of $57.83, that has come into possession of defendant since the present officers were elected or placed in charge of the business of defendant." Apparently, these three officers came into office not knowing that the court had issued a previous order to hand over Sandlin's money. Sandlin insisted that he was still owed $1,464.19 with 6% interest from January 1, 1930, until paid. The Plaintiff stated that on May 10, 1935, the VFW paid him $57.83 and that the VFW should be given a credit for this amount against the original amount of $1,464.19. Thus, Sandlin argued that the VFW had paid him nothing except the $57.83. This document also stated that Mr. Sandlin had obtained a new attorney, Mr. M. C. Begley. [10]

Through his attorney, Sandlin insisted that he did not, "authorize defendant to invest his money in such property [the 120 shares of bank stock] and if defendant did, as it claims, invest his money in these shares, it did so without his consent and without authority." Furthermore, Sandlin argued that he did not own the stock since he had not authorized its purchase, he wanted the court to order it sold and a lien placed on it, and the proceeds from the sale applied to the money the VFW owed Sandlin.

A lien is a document filed in the courthouse placing the world on notice that one person owes another person money. The lien will attach or apply to a very specific piece of property. In the event that the specific piece of property is sold, the proceeds from the sale will be used to pay the person who is owed money. The effect of this was that if the 120 shares of stock had been sold, then the proceeds would have been used to pay Sandlin monies he alleged the VFW owed him. Of course, a court must make this determination, further complicating procedures which would wind their way through a lawsuit and cause further delay. [11]

Sandlin's efforts to recoup this money from the VFW were made much more difficult by the financial circumstances of the 1930s. Following the stock market crash of 1929, Americans began withdrawing their money from banks all across the country. In 1930, approximately 24,000 banks operated in the United States. Eight thousand (8,000) banks belonged to the Federal Reserve System which was established in 1914 for the purpose of establishing public confidence in the nation's banks and ensuring their solvency. However, approximately 16,000 other banks

STILL TRYING FOR FINANCIAL ASSISTANCE IN THE 1930s

did not belong to the Federal Reserve System. These banks operated under rules that required them to have sufficient money in the bank, called reserve funds, so they could pay depositors in the event they made a run on the banks.

Two problems made it difficult for these banks to retain sufficient funds to pay all their depositors. First, banks counted their reserve funds as cash on hand plus any checks they had in the bank. These checks, called the "float," did not represent cash on hand. They represented potential cash that could be withdrawn from another bank. When people made a demand for their money, the banks could only pay them with the cash on hand. Since there was not enough cash to satisfy the demands of the depositors, the bank failed. Second, the banks could deposit some of their funds in other banks, and then draw upon them to give them the cash they needed when depositors were demanding their money. Since the other banks could count their "float" as a part of their cash on hand, they failed to have sufficient funds to pay the first bank when it demanded its money. As a result, many banks failed simultaneously. [12]

Finally, on April 23, 1937, a court judgement said:

> *"It is further agreed and adjudged by the court that the plaintiff Willie Sandlin, is the owner and is adjudged to be the owner of the 120 corporate trust share[s] (modified) consisting of 100 shares certificates No. 14612, 10 shares MLB, 19637, and 10 shares M1 19638, and also the owner and entitled to proceeds of one liquidating agents, certificate of proof of claim of union centereael [central] Bank Louisville, Kentucky, No, 526.*
>
> *In addition to the above the plaintiff Willie Sandlin accepts the sum of $500.00 as a full and complete settlement of this case, and as heretofore agreed, the case is now dismissed and settled."*

This order and judgement indicated that Sandlin finally accepted the corporate stock of 120 shares. The national economy had improved by the late

SERGEANT SANDLIN

1930s, and laws were in place to insure solvency of the nation's banks. By 1937, the value of this stock had apparently improved and Sandlin was willing to accept it as a partial payment of the money that was due him. The Union Central Bank certified that it had a specific amount of money in the VFW account for Sandlin. The settlement order did not specify how much the certified amount was, but it was sufficient to satisfy Sandlin and his attorney as evidenced by Attorney Begley's signature on behalf of his client. In addition, Sandlin was to receive $500 in cash. [13]

Although the court ruled on Sandlin's behalf, this episode in Sandlin's life did not have a happy ending. Further examination of the Circuit Court Records for Leslie County revealed no additional references to this case. If he did not receive his money from the VFW, he could have requested additional action on his behalf from the court. No additional mention of this case in the court records could mean two things: the matter was satisfactorily resolved or Willie simply gave up. Sandlin's widow and daughter both later declared that Willie never received a penny of the money that the VFW collected on his behalf. [14]

In spite of his poor health and financial problems, Willie remained a positive leader and provided a spirit of optimism in his community. In 1930, representative Elmer J. Terry of Breathitt County introduced a bill to provide a $75,000 appropriation for a library to be constructed in Jackson, the county seat. The library "would be designated as a World War memorial in honor of Kentucky soldiers killed in the war and Sergeant Willie Sandlin," one of the heroes of the Great War. Breathitt County was the only county in the United States that did not have to draft men for service in World War I, because the county's quota was continually filled by volunteers. This fact would be commemorated by a special bronze plaque on the building if the proposed measure passed. Although Hiram Brock's bill to provide a home for Sandlin never passed the Kentucky legislature, Sandlin generously lent his name and support to the library project. "Bloody Breathitt," one of Kentucky's feud counties, was to be memorialized by a public building containing a public library,

STILL TRYING FOR FINANCIAL ASSISTANCE IN THE 1930s

a museum, and a "special tablet" honoring Willie Sandlin. Terry's bill was approved by the legislature on May 13, 1930, and awaited the approval of Governor Flem D. Sampson. [15]

Increasing Health Problems

Sandlin's life in the 1930s continued to be a series of medical examinations. He was examined at Cincinnati in 1928 and given a 69 percent disability rating, which would have entitled him to a fair compensation. But the Louisville Veterans' Bureau, which had jurisdiction over Sandlin, appealed that rating to the Bureau of Appeals at Chicago and the bureau then placed the case before the Veterans' Bureau in Washington. Bureaucracies do not always yield justice, and, although the bureau had always been very sympathetic toward Sandlin's case, technicalities blocked compensation for him, making a special action by Congress necessary. Willie was still waiting, in 1928, nine years after he mustered out. In 1932, he was examined at the U.S. Veterans Bureau in Lexington, and again doctors reported that he had suffered lung damage from being gassed, but no financial assistance emerged from this exam. [16]

Health problems plagued him for the remainder of his life. For example, he wrote to the Veterans Administration office in Louisville about benefits and he was advised that "the purpose of this office" was "to review those cases acted upon previous to the receipt of recent instructions from Central Office." The Adjudication Officer, N.E. Whiting, advised Sandlin that his case "will therefore be reconsidered in its order and as soon as definitive action has been taken thereon you will be promptly advised of the decision made." [17] Two years later, Sandlin was still waiting for a decision on his V.A. benefits. He was admitted to a Diagnostic Center in Hines, Illinois, by the Louisville Regional Office on December 5, 1935 and discharged December 30, 1935, "by reason of Observation Completed." [18]

VETERANS ADMINISTRATION
Louisville, Kentucky,
June 7, 1933.

YOUR FILE REFERENCE:

IN REPLY REFER TO:
C-228 151   .422

Mr. Willie Sandlin,
Hyden,
Kentucky.

Dear Sir:

This will acknowledge receipt of your letter dated May 26, 1933 in which you request information relative to a recent rating made in your case under the provisions of the recent Act of Congress, approved March 20, 1933.

You are advised it is the purpose of this office to again review those cases acted upon previous to the receipt of recent instructions from Central Office. Your case will therefore be reconsidered in its order and as soon as definite action has been taken thereon you will be promptly advised of the decision made.

In future correspondence regarding this case, refer to C-228 151.

By direction,

N. E. Whiting
N. E. WHITING
Adjudication Officer.

Willie Sandlin, a twice-wounded, twice-gassed Medal of Honor recipient, never received a penny from the Veterans Administration. *Florence Muncy Collection.*

**VETERANS ADMINISTRATION
DIAGNOSTIC CENTER
HINES, ILLINOIS**

EDWARD HINES JR. CENTER

Discharge Certificate

This is to certify that   WILLIE SANDLIN

C-228 151   was admitted to this Diagnostic Center   Dec. 5, 1935
                                                      DATE

by the   Louisville, Ky.   Regional Office

under the provisions of the World War Veterans' Act,

Section   Medical Directors Letter of Oct. 10, 1935

and was discharged   Dec. 30, 1935   by reason of
                     DATE

Observation Completed.

He was not absent without permission and had no restrictions.

Chas F Ensign
Reception Officer.

Approved:
John B Anderson
Chief Diagnostic Center.

Willie Sandlin
Patient's Signature.

Throughout the 1920s and 1930s, Sandlin sought V. A. compensation and visited V. A. diagnostic centers on a regular basis. *Florence Muncy Collection.*

SERGEANT SANDLIN

War Clouds on the Horizon

Trying to recover from the depression, America adopted an isolationist foreign policy in the 1930s. With the horrors of World War I fresh in their minds, Americans were quick to say: "Let Europe stew in its own juices." While America focused on the economic recovery brought about by New Deal policies and programs, European and Asian dictators saw an opportunity for aggressive expansion that soon challenged the world order. The first major aggression of the 1930s came in 1931 when Japan seized Manchuria. In 1935, Mussolini's Italy invaded Ethiopia. At the same time, in defiance of the peace treaty that ended World War I, Germany began to rebuild its war machine. In 1936, German troops occupied the Rhineland, in defiance of the Treaty of Versailles. By 1937, the aggressive nations of German, Italy, and Japan had allied themselves against Great Britain and other western powers. America's diplomatic posture was to stay out of war, rather than to keep war from happening. By 1937, President Roosevelt realized that America had ignored the Axis Powers for too long. He recognized a "spreading epidemic of world lawlessness" and suggested that aggressors be "quarantined." The Axis Powers were undeterred by words. By 1938, Japan had taken over China. That same year, Hitler's troops took control of Austria and began threatening to absorb Czechoslovakia. The next year Hitler took over Czechoslovakia, invaded Albania, and threatened Poland. By then it was obvious that only war would stop the aggression of these three powers. After Germany invaded Poland, Great Britain and France declared war on Germany. In 1939, Sandlin's VFW group, the Hugh McKee Post No. 677, met at the Drake Hotel in Lexington and unanimously adopted a resolution "expressing their determination to volunteer for service immediately in the event the United States enters the present European war." Copies of the resolution were sent to President Roosevelt, the Secretary of War, and the Secretary of the Navy. [19] By 1940, France had surrendered to Hitler's invading armies, and only Britain stood against Germany's

Peacetime conscription was introduced in the United States for the first time in 1940. Recruiting posters, like the one shown here, encouraged volunteers to join all branches of the armed forces.

Army recruiting poster. On December 29, 1940, President Roosevelt told the nation, "We must be the great arsenal of democracy." A year later, Japanese airplanes bombed Pearl Harbor. The beginning of another World War stirred vivid memories held by Willie Sandlin and millions of other veterans of the Great War.

STILL TRYING FOR FINANCIAL ASSISTANCE IN THE 1930s

plans for world domination. The Roosevelt administration tried to help the British but remain out of the war – an awkward stance. Finally, war came to our doorsteps. On December 7, 1941, Japanese planes attacked and severely crippled the American fleet at Pearl Harbor. The next day, Congress declared war.

While these major events were taking place, Willie Sandlin and his Leslie County neighbors paid little attention to the crisis in Europe and the impending world war. Leslie Countians knew what was happening abroad, but it seemed irrelevant to their lives. Still mired in depression-decade difficulties, the people of Leslie County – like the majority of people in Central and Southern Appalachia – ignored the European crisis. Somehow war in Europe was not Leslie County's problem! Leslie Countians were more interested in local news like the "outstanding event of the year in Leslie County" – the occupation of the new home economics practice house, made by partitioning the former public high school building. "It is not ideally furnished, but is quite livable and the girls are receiving the kind of training that will do them good all their lives." All of this was being done under the supervision of Miss Leota Sullinger, the high school home economics teacher. Also of local interest was the death of Mrs. Clark Napier of Hyden who was bitten by a rattlesnake during a religious service. Leslie County Judge Boone Begley fined the snake's owner, Lige Bowling, $50 on a charge that he violated a 1940 statute prohibiting the use of reptiles in religious services. [20]

But a peacetime draft got their attention! In September 1940, the first peacetime Selective Service Act in American history was signed after lengthy congressional debate. All men between the ages of 21 and 36 had to register. That amounted to more than 10% of Leslie County's population. Who would do the work if the men of Leslie County went to war? Even the old warrior Willie Sandlin, who was 52 years old, registered on April 26, 1942. Sandlin told members of the Hugh McKee VFW Post that "he expected Army officials to accept his offer " [for military service]. Because Sandlin expected to return to some form of military service, he also reported that he was planning to "move to Lexington within a few weeks so that he [could] enroll his five children in

SERGEANT SANDLIN

Willie Sandlin went to Hyden and registered for the draft on April 26, 1942. He was 52 years old and in bad health, and he was married with five children. He was willing to serve again, but he was physically unable.

school." [21] Coincidentally, one day after Sandlin registered, Alvin York did the same thing. "Eager for a combat role," York, overweight and arthritic, registered "in the same general store where he had registered twenty-five years earlier." The "army denied him regular military service." [22]

Four days after the Japanese attack on Pearl Harbor, the Leslie County newspaper devoted one-sixth of the front page – a single column of text – announcing that "a state of war existed" between the United States and Japan as a result of the "sudden and dastardly acts upon our island possessions which occurred December 7." The newspaper also noted that on that day, December 11, Germany and Italy had declared war against the United States and that our country had reciprocated with a declaration of war. [23]

We are the Dead. Short days ago
We lived, felt dawn, saw sunset glow
Loved and were loved, and now we lie
In Flanders fields.

"In Flanders Fields"
Lieut. Col. John McCrae

CHAPTER TEN
THE 1940S: A WAR HERO'S DEATH

The new decade of the 1940s brought an almost palpable sense of relief to Willie Sandlin and his Leslie County friends and neighbors. They had survived the depression decade and the economy was improving. Sandlin had just turned fifty years old. He had been happily married for twenty years, and he had four children still living at home. Willie was still working at the WPA job; the federal census listed him as a government worker with property valued at $1000 and an eighth-grade education.

On December 22, 1941, fifteen days after the day the Japanese attacked Pearl Harbor, Belvia's father died at the age of 79 and left his large farm in equal shares to three of his children: Belvia and her two brothers, Watt and Golden. He gave land in another part of Leslie County to his other three surviving children. In his death notice, he was praised as a "prominent citizen who was head of the Telephone Company in this county for many years. Funeral services were held at his home with Dr. F. C. Symonds in charge. The Masonic Lodge of Hyden conducted the services at the cemetery." Roberts was survived by his

William Roberts' death certificate. Willie's father-in-law left one-third of his farm to Willie and Belvia. Although William Roberts' obituary said he died on December 22, 1941, his death certificate said he died on December 7, 1941, the day that the Japanese attacked Pearl Harbor.

THE 1940s: A WAR HERO'S DEATH

wife, Sally Ann, and six children: sons Ottis, Watt, and Golden and daughters Mrs. Willie Sandlin of Hyden, Mrs. Sophia Cook of Loyal, Kentucky, and Mrs. Cal Nantz of Laurel County. [1] William Roberts was buried in the family cemetery on a hill overlooking his home, the same cemetery where two of Willie and Belvia's daughters were buried.

Willie and Belvia received the bottom land near the river, so they could grow corn. William's widow, Sally Ann, continued to live in the "big house," and her son, Watt, who never married, lived with her. Watt sold his share of the land inheritance to Willie and Belvia, so they owned two-thirds of the farm where Belvia had been raised.

In December 1941, John F. Day and a friend called on Willie, Belvia, and their children at their home. They drove about a mile down-river from Hyden "along a WPA road that Sandlin helped build when he was a project supervisor." After Day parked his car, he and his companion crossed the middle fork of the Kentucky river by "leaping from stone to stone" because there was no bridge. Once across, they walked up a creek bed for about 200 yards to the stone house that Willie had built for his family almost a decade earlier.

Willie greeted them with "a hearty welcome" at his door, apologizing for his unkempt appearance by explaining that he had been sick for several days and that his breathing problems had become "so bad for a spell I thought I was shorley going out."

His visitors described Willie as a "heavyset" man of average height with brown eyes and a "mop of dark hair just tinged with gray." "When he laughs," said Day, "he laughs all over, throwing back his head and showing two gold teeth."

Willie, Belvia, and their guests sat comfortably in "a long living room" and talked about "a number of things," but soon the conversation turned to Japan's attack on Pearl Harbor and America's entrance into another world war. While Willie refused to talk about his heroics in World War I, he told his visitors that if his health were better and if "the navy would take [me, I would] join

SERGEANT SANDLIN

tomorrow." Willie Sandlin, an army veteran who received the Medal of Honor for heroics against the German army in September 1918, was prepared to serve his country again! Day would later write: "That's right, he's an army man, but he'd like a go at the navy." While the men were talking about war, Belvia quietly excused herself and returned carrying Willie's army coat with his medals.

"I thought you-all'd be interested in seeing these," Belvia explained, ignoring Willie's obvious embarrassment.

After dragging a few reluctant comments from Willie about his accomplishments, Mr. Day said, "You must have been very proud."

"Aw, it wasn't much. Anyway, you can't eat medals." Then Willie laughed and suggested that his guests join the family for supper. [2]

Willie's cousin, "Merdie" Morris, said Willie had terrible breathing problems in the 1940s and suffered "seizures" for about three years – sometimes the seizures came "one after another." When Merdie saw him in 1947, Willie "wheezed bad and did not have wind." [3] In spite of health problems, Willie Sandlin remained an involved and loving parent. When his youngest daughter Florence married in 1946, Willie walked his daughter up the church aisle. Before he returned to his seat, he told the groom – in a clear voice – "If you ever harm a hair on her head, I will kill you." [4]

Willie also remained an active member of the Hyden/Leslie County community. During World War II, Sandlin contributed his time and efforts to several forms of community service. In 1944, President Franklin D. Roosevelt signed a Certificate of Award from the Office of Price Administration acknowledging Sandlin's "meritorious service" to the price and rationing programs. Sandlin also served on Leslie County's Selective Service Board. [5] He served as Commander of the American Legion post in Leslie County for several years and "was a leader of the Young Democrats Club in Leslie County," as well as an active participant in the veterans division of the Democratic campaign organization. [6]

In 1941, Sandlin's health was declining, but he still had a large family to

Willie and Belvia, Spring 1941. *Photo courtesy of Leona Nichols*

Belvia and her daughters, Spring 1947. Belvia (top). Second Row, Vorres (left; Nancy Ruth (right). Bottom Row, Florence (left); Leona (right). Nancy was pregnant with the child who would grow up to be Lue Peabody. Lue has made a splendid contribution to this book by submitting her Aunt Leona's photos and memories. *Photo courtesy of Leona Nichols.*

During World War II, Sandlin served for five years on Leslie County's draft board. The mountain counties usually met their quotas with a high incidence of volunteerism, but some mountain boys were drafted. For example, the famous author James Still was the oldest man drafted from nearby Knott County and served with the army in North Africa.

"IN KENTUCKY"

BY
JUDGE JAMES HILLARY MULLIGAN

The moonlight falls the softest
    In Kentucky;
The summer's days come oft'est
    In Kentucky;
Friendship is the strongest;
Love's fires glow the longest;
Yet, a wrong is always wrongest
    In Kentucky.

The sunshine's ever brightest
    In Kentucky;
The breezes whisper lightest
    In Kentucky;
Plain girls are the fewest,
Maidens' eyes the bluest,
Their little hearts are truest
    In Kentucky.

Life's burdens bear the lightest
    In Kentucky;
The home fires burn the brightest
    In Kentucky;
While prayers are the keenest,
Cards come out the meanest,
The pocket empties cleanest
    In Kentucky.

Orators are the grandest
    In Kentucky;
Officials are the blandest
    In Kentucky;
Boys are all the fliest,
Danger ever nighest,
Taxes are the highest
    In Kentucky.

The bluegrass waves the bluest
    In Kentucky;
Yet bluebloods are the fewest
    In Kentucky;
Moonshine is the clearest,
By no means the dearest,
And yet it acts the queerest,
    In Kentucky.

The dove's notes are the saddest
    In Kentucky;
The streams dance on the gladdest
    In Kentucky;
Hip pockets are the thickest,
Pistol hands the slickest,
The cylinder turns the quickest
    In Kentucky.

Song birds are the sweetest
    In Kentucky;
The thoroughbreds the fleetest
    In Kentucky;
Mountains tower proudest,
Thunder peals the loudest,
The landscape is the grandest –
And politics – the damnedest
    In Kentucky.

James Hillary Mulligan (1844-1915) graduated from St. Mary's College in 1864 and received his law degree from Kentucky University in 1869. Editor, attorney, judge, state senator, consul-general to Somoa, and orator, Judge Mulligan wrote "In Kentucky," perhaps the best-known poem about the state. His home, Maxwell Place, is now the official residence of the president of the University of Kentucky. Willie Sandlin was a hard-working farmer with a large family to support, and he had neither the time nor the inclination to read poetry. However, after his losing campaign to serve as Leslie County's jailer (see pages 202-203), he probably would have agreed with Judge James Hillary Mulligan that "politics was the damnedest in Kentucky."

support. So, for the first time in his life, Willie sought political office. He ran as an Independent for Leslie County jailer. Sandlin, an ardent Democrat, had not lost the "spirit of battle" when he attempted to wrest this elected office from a Republican nominee in Leslie County, "the banner Republican county in the state." Leslie County had never elected an official representing the Democratic Party, prompting Willie to run as an Independent.

Sandlin ran for Leslie County jailer in 1941 and lost.

He was very well liked, his only "drawback . . . being his political affiliation." Perhaps this honored veteran "likes a fight better than he does an office," observed Ray Huff of Combs, Kentucky. "If he had changed his politics, his election to any office in this county would have been a forgone conclusion." But Sandlin held honor over expediency and placed himself in a no-win situation. He did not win, but he drew much support and approval for his determined campaign.[7]

After the election, Sandlin published a letter in the local newspaper thanking his friends who voted for him and supported his campaign. "I can never do as much for you as I would like to do," he wrote. "And you will always be remembered by my family and me." Sandlin's explanation for his loss offers keen insight into his determined character:

THE 1940s: A WAR HERO'S DEATH

I would like to explain to those who don't know that a bunch of selfish politicians around Hyden have pooled a sum of money together and defeated me. I wish to forgive them for their activity. [8]

During the 1940s, the VFW continued its unsuccessful efforts to secure financial assistance for Sandlin. In May 1942, the Lexington post "suggested to high government officials" that Sandlin "be commissioned an officer in the army." [9]

Willie Sandlin's Death

Early in May 1949, Willie's breathing problems grew much worse. Belvia took him to the hospital in Hyden; two days later his daughter Leona and her husband, George Asher, took him to the Veteran's Hospital in Louisville. Belvia went with him and stayed in the hospital room for the next three weeks.

In the early morning hours of May 29, Belvia was sitting next to Willie's bed and holding his hand. Doctors had advised Willie to move to Phoenix. They thought the climate and environment there might improve his health. He squeezed her hand and said, "We missed the train [to Phoenix]." And then he was dead. He went easy, with a smile and a sigh. Some might have thought it was just his final breath. Others, more atuned to the infinite, might have heard him whisper: "I am Willie Sandlin. When I was in the forests of France, my heart was in the hills of Kentucky."

He answered his last roll call on this earth at age 59 at 8:30 am in the V. A. (Nichols) Hospital in Louisville on May 29, 1949. He died from a lingering lung infection attributed to German poison gas attacks in France's Argonne Forest. Sandlin's official death record indicates that he died from Pulmonary Emphysema and Hypertensive Cardiovascular disease. [10] He was originally buried in Hurricane Cemetery near Hyden. Belvia, who was physically and

Willie Sandlin's death certificate. He died in the V. A. Hospital in Louisville on May 29, 1949. He was 59 years old.

THE 1940s: A WAR HERO'S DEATH

emotionally exhausted from her husband's death, passed out at the funeral. She was taken by ambulance to the hospital in Hyden and remained there for three days before returning home. "He was our hero; he was the whole family's hero," said his daughters. "When we were small, we didn't know much about the war, but he was our hero always." Willie was survived by his wife, Belvia, five children, three brothers, John, Charlie, and Mathew, one half-sister, Mrs. Doshia Gabbard of McKee, Kentucky, and five grandchildren. [11]

Sandlin's death brought tributes from across Kentucky and across America. *The Louisville Courier-Journal* editorial captured Sandlin's greatness:

> *Sergeant Sandlin came back to the Kentucky mountains a famous man and spent the rest of his life ignoring and refusing to capitalize on his fame. He farmed as his neighbors did in the Leslie County hills, until poor health made the hard work impossible. His children remained, as he did, a part of the community in which they were born.*
>
> *All of Kentucky has a right to be proud of Sergeant Sandlin, but his qualities were typically those of the mountain Kentuckian, who is slow to anger, contemptuous of the enticements of big cities, and fantastically brave in danger. Eastern Kentucky may well mourn her native son, but there are others like him in the hills.*

The Lexington Leader said it was "fitting that his death occurred as the nation was observing Memorial Day." Sergeant Sandlin's name had become "a synonym for personal bravery," observed the paper, and "his name is symbolic of the patriotism and stoutheartedness of the mountain people." The story of his deed "had become a part of the history of the nation," yet Sandlin's heroics were not rewarded during his lifetime and he became little more than a footnote in Kentucky history as the twentieth century progressed. [12]

APPLICATION FOR HEADSTONE OR MARKER

BORN - Ky. (over)

ORIGINAL

CHECK TYPE REQUIRED: ☒ UPRIGHT MARBLE HEADSTONE

ENLISTMENT DATE: April 17, 1919 17
DISCHARGE DATE: May 30, 1919 Hon.
SERIAL No.: 2 078 103
PENSION No.: 228 151
STATE: Ky / Arizona
RANK: Sgt.
COMPANY: A
EMBLEM: ☒ CHRISTIAN

NAME: SANDLIN, Willie
U.S. REGIMENT, STATE ORGANIZATION, AND DIVISION: 132nd Inf. 33rd Div.
DATE OF BIRTH: January 1, 1890
DATE OF DEATH: May 29, 1949
NAME OF CEMETERY: Sandlin Cemetery
LOCATION: Hyden, Kentucky
SIGNATURE OF CONSIGNEE: Belvia Sandlin
NEAREST FREIGHT STATION: Hazard, Ky
POST OFFICE ADDRESS OF CONSIGNEE: Hyden, Ky

FOR VERIFICATION: JUN 24 1949
ORDERED: Tate, Ga. 9 AUG 1949
B/L: 6345038

APPLICANT'S SIGNATURE: Belvia Sandlin
ADDRESS: Hyden, Ky.

OQMG FORM 623 REV 15 APR 47   AGRS DW-M 7 July 49 HH

Enl. 17 Apr. 1913 Disch. 16 Apr. 1917 - Hon. - Cpl. - Co "H" 35th Inf.
Was awarded the Congressional Medal of Honor.

I HEREBY CERTIFY that the type headstone or marker requested by the applicant will be permitted at the grave. (Be sure you have noted what type is indicated by applicant on form)

Leslie County Cemetery Association
(Signature of superintendent, sexton, or caretaker)

Date: June 13, 1949

RECEIVED JUN 15 1949

Return to: OFFICE OF THE QUARTERMASTER GENERAL,
MEMORIAL DIVISION,
WASHINGTON 25, D. C.

After Willie's death, Belvia applied for and received a military headstone for Willie's grave.

RESOLUTION

WHEREAS, on Sunday, May 29th, 1949, our beloved and most faithful comrade, Willie Sandlin answered his last Roll Call on this earth and joined other comrades in that place set apart to the real veterans who have fought to keep our country free.

Willie Sandlin enlisted in the Regular Army April 17, 1913, served on the Mexican Border in 1916; served overseas with the 33rd Division in France; was one of the few to be awarded the Congressional Medal of Honor for his unsurpassed feat of filling twenty-four Germans single handed in one day, and, according to the official record, of all men who were awarded such a medal, he was the greatest of all. He was known as the most modest hero of the First World War, and consistently, to the last, refused to accept many lucrative offers to commercialize on his deeds as a soldier.

He returned home and on July third, 1924 became a member of Hugh McKee Post No. 677, Veterans of Foreign Wars, the oldest Post in Kentucky, and also known throughout the United States as having more decorated veterans as members than any other Post in the National Organization. He served as Chief of Staff for the Department of Kentucky a number of terms and at the time of his death had served for over twenty years as Aide-de-Camp to the Commander-in-Chief, Medal of Honor Class. He represented the Post at National Conventions throughout the country for several years, and brought not only to his Post, but to all Kentucky, more honor and renoun than any single man for many years.

NOW, BE IT RESOLVED: by Hugh McKee Post No. 677, Lexington, Kentucky, that this Post has lost its most valuable member, and the most decorated one, as well as one of the best workers; that a copy of this Resolution be spread upon the Minutes of the Post; a copy to his family; to Foreign Service, and to the two Lexington newspapers, the Louisville, Kentucky papers, and the newspaper at Hyden, Kentucky, and that the Charter of the Post be draped for thirty days.

COMMITTEE

R. E. Lee Murphy, Past Department Commander.

Taylor N. House, Past Commander

Kelley G. Rogers, Member of Committee.

Roger F. Mulloy, Commander

Following Sandlin's death, the Hugh McKee Post No. 677 in Lexington passed a formal Resolution honoring the life and accomplishments of its "most valuable member."

SERGEANT SANDLIN

Following Sandlin's death, the Hugh-McKee Post 677 in Lexington, Kentucky, published a lengthy resolution that the Post had "lost its most valuable member." The Hyden Masonic Number 664 published a similar resolution about losing "a true and faithful brother." Those resolutions, along with the family's public letter of thanks are included in Appendix B.

Now he belongs to the ages. He had been raised in poverty and had grown into a quiet, resolute man of courage and honor. All he wanted from life was to serve his country, build a home, and enjoy his loving family, and he achieved his goals through hard work. Only death can stop men like Willie Sandlin.

To the vile dust from whence he sprung
Unwept, unhonored, and unsung.

"Love of Country"
Sir Walter Scott

CHAPTER ELEVEN
A HERO'S LEGACY

Posthumous Recognition

After Willie died, he was not buried in the Roberts family cemetery, near Nanny and Pap and his two daughters, Cora and Rose, who had both died as children. The Roberts family cemetery was on a high hill overlooking their home. At the time of Willie's death, there was no road leading to the family cemetery, which was accessible only by walking a steep and narrow path. So Willie was buried in the Hurricane Cemetery in Hyden. The Masonic Lodge held services, and Reverend Benton P. Deaton spoke words of comfort to the bereaved at the funeral services in the high school auditorium prior to the burial. Nearly one thousand people attended the services. [1]

During his lifetime, Sandlin had refused to accept the public recognition that should have fallen to one of our nation's greatest heroes, but he has since received a great deal of posthumous recognition. On June 5, 1964, Kentucky Highway Historical Marker Number 631 – honoring Sergeant Willie Sandlin – was installed on the courthouse grounds in Willie's hometown, Hyden. The

Kentucky Highway Historical Marker Number 631 – honoring Willie Sandlin – stands near the Leslie County courthouse in Hyden. *Photo courtesy of Wayne Onkst.*

A HERO'S LEGACY

Willie's daughter Florence and his widow Belvia attend the ceremony on September 17, 1975, when the United States Army Reserve Training Center in Hyden was named for Willie Sandlin. *Florence Muncy Collection.*

years ahead would bring more honors.

On September 17, 1975, the United States Army Reserve Training Center in Hyden was dedicated in his memory. Speakers at the dedication ceremony included Kentucky Governor Julian Carroll, Senator Wendell Ford, Congressman Carl D. Perkins, and other political and civic leaders. Belvia was on the speaker's stand, too, and she told the assemblage how honored she and her family felt to see Willie Sandlin recognized. On that same day, Willie was honored by Hyden's Masonic Lodge Number 664, which praised his life accomplishments and also recognized his valuable service to his Lodge and the

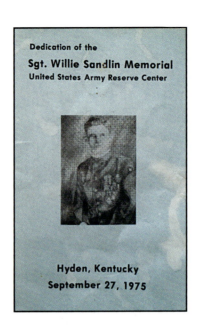

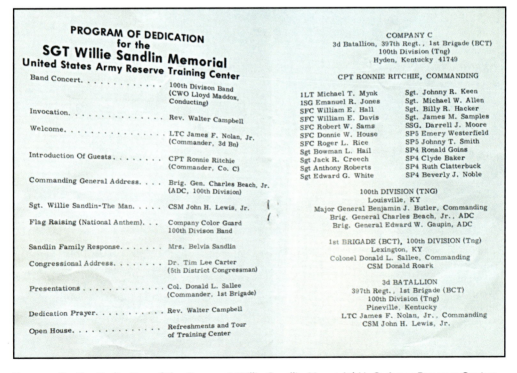

Program for the Dedication of the Sergeant Willie Sandlin Memorial U. S. Army Reserve Center. Speakers at the ceremony included Kentucky Governor Julian Carroll, Senator Wendell Ford, and Congressman Carl Perkins. *Sandlin Family Collection.*

A HERO'S LEGACY

The Willie Sandlin Pool in Hyden. *Florence Muncy Collection.*

Masonic Fraternity. Later, a local swimming pool was named in his honor.

For the remainder of the twentieth century, Sandlin continued to receive posthumous honors and recognitions. On August 14, 1976, he was recognized on the Kentucky obelisk in the Medal of Honor Grove by the Freedom Foundation in Valley Forge, Pennsylvania. Willie's widow Belvia and other family members attended. Fifteen years later, with the ceremonial assistance of the American Legion, Belvia and her children were present when Willie's body was removed from the Hurricane Cemetery in Hyden and reinterred in the Zachary Taylor National Cemetery in Louisville, Kentucky. [2] Almost a decade later, on May 28, 1999, Willie was recognized on the National Medal of Honor Memorial in Indianapolis, Indiana.

Leslie County's modest war hero continued to receive posthumous honors into the twenty-first century. On November 12, 2001, Sandlin was recognized on the Kentucky Medal of Honor Memorial in Louisville, Kentucky. The Blue Grass Army Depot Headquarters was named for Willie in July 2008. In March

Official ceremonies at the Leslie County High School on September 17, 1975 when the U.S. Army Reserve Training Center was named for Willie Sandlin. *Florence Muncy Collection.*

2012, Governor Steve Beshear joined lawmakers and veterans groups from across Kentucky to unveil a bronze plaque listing the name of Sergeant Willie Sandlin among Kentucky's 60 Medal of Honor recipients. (See Appendix C) The plaque hangs in the Capitol Rotunda, opposite the statue of Abraham Lincoln, whose administration worked with Congress to create the Medal of Honor in 1862 to recognize valor during the Civil War. On June 24, 2016, the Sergeant Willie Sandlin Memorial Bridge was dedicated on Kentucky Route 30, near the intersection of Kentucky Route 3237 in Breathitt County. [3]

In retrospect, it was too little and too late for a great war hero who died in obscurity of war-inflicted wounds.

Belvia attends the dedication of the Kentucky obelisk in the Medal of Honor Grove of the Freedom Foundation in Valley Forge, Pennsylvania. *Florence Muncy Collection.*

Belvia helps to plant a tree in the Medal of Honor Grove in Valley Forge, Pennsylvania. *Florence Muncy Collection.*

In 1991, Belvia and her children had Willie's body moved from the Hurricane Cemetery in Hyden to the Zachary Taylor National Cemetery in Louisville. From the left, Nancy Ruth, Leona, Belvia and Florence. Robert and Vorres are in the back. *Florence Muncy Collection.*

The American Legion assists with Willie's reinterment. *Florence Muncy Collection.*

Willie is immortalized on the National Medal of Honor Memorial in Indianapolis, Indiana.
Photo courtesy of John Trowbridge.

In 2008, the Blue Grass Army Depot in Richmond dedicated the headquarters as Sandlin Hall in honor of Sgt. Willie Sandlin, the only Kentuckian to receive the Congressional Medal of Honor in World War I. The bronze relief of Sandlin was unveiled by Brigadier General James E. Rogers (left) and Col. Richard J. Mason Jr. *The Lexington Herald-Leader.*

The Kentucky Medal of Honor Memorial is located at the corner of Fifth and Jefferson Streets in downtown Louisville, on the grounds of the old Jefferson County courthouse. The Memorial honors all of Kentucky's recipients of the Medal of Honor.
Photo courtesy of John Trowbridge.

The Kentucky Medal of Honor Memorial was sculpted by Doyle Glass and dedicated on Veterans Day 2001. The Memorial features a life-size bronze statue of Medal of Honor recipient John C. Squires of Louisville who was killed in action in Italy during World War II.
Photo courtesy of John Trowbridge.

A plaque on the base of the Kentucky Medal of Honor Memorial lists each of the sixty recipients of the Medal of Honor. Those names are listed in Appendix C. *Photo courtesy of John Trowbridge.*

Family dinner, Christmas 1990. Back row, Florence, Vorres, Bob, and Leona. Nancy and Belvia are seated. *Photo courtesy of Leona Nichols.*

> Special thanks to the following persons who contributed to the section entitled "Willie Sandlin's Family Legacy": Leona Sandlin Nichols, Florence Sandlin Muncy, Gloria Jean Day, Carol Lee Day Deffinger, Philip Sandlin, Lue Dena Asher Peabody, Donna Haga.

Willie Sandlin's Family Legacy

Willie's wife, Belvia Roberts Sandlin, lived almost 50 more years after his death, and she never married again. She had been living with her daughter Florence in St. Matthews, a suburb of Louisville, when she died at the age of 96. Her daughters spoke often of her happy marriage and said their parents' "love and respect had lasted their lifetime on this earth."

Belvia had moved to Louisville in 1951 to be near her only son, Robert E. Lee Sandlin, who was in pharmacy school. Willie had been dead for three years and Belvia was no longer content to live in Leslie County because she missed Willie so much. She and Willie had twenty-nine good years together in their hand-hewn stone house on Owl's Nest Creek. Her daughters said Belvia "was as much of a hero as Willie because of all her good deeds." For example, the Sandlins often kept students "who had no way into town" in their home so they could attend high school. Also, when new midwife trainees arrived at the Mary Breckinridge Hospital, Belvia often prepared meals for them. After Willie died, Belvia continued to fight for rights which had been denied her late husband. For example, on December 22, 1961, Belvia finally received the $500 bonus which Willie had applied for when he returned from France in 1919 and should have received on his birthday in 1945.

Throughout her long life, Belvia remained devoted to her husband's heroic legacy. Over the years, time had faded the neck ribbon of Sandlin's Medal of Honor. Belvia made "numerous attempts to secure a new one," with no success until a close friend, Kentucky National Guard Warrant Officer Wilbur Kirk, learned of her efforts. Kirk brought the matter to the attention of Kentucky Adjutant General, Major Billy G. Wellman, and U.S. Senator Wendell Ford. At the Kentucky National Guard Open House on May 21, 1983, General Wellman presented Belvia with a new neck ribbon and a Kentucky Colonel Certificate. Later that afternoon, members of the Kentucky National Guard re-enacted Willie

SERGEANT SANDLIN

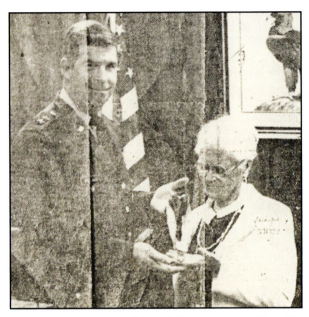

At the Kentucky National Guard Open House on Mary 21, 1983, Adjutant General Billy Wellman presented Belvia with a new neck ribbon for Willie's Medal of Honor. *Florence Muncy Collection.*

Sandlin's heroic assault on three German machine gun nests. "Now," reflected Belvia, "I think I know what Willie went through." [4]

At her death, Belvia was a member of the Hyden Presbyterian Church, Sojourners Lodge at Fort Knox, Order of the Eastern Star, and Frontier Nursing Service in Hyden. A splendid wife, mother, grandmother, and friend, Belvia was survived by three of her daughters – Leona, Florence, and Vorres, 17 grandchildren, 14 great-grandchildren, and six great-great-grandchildren. [5]

Willie and Belvia had seven children, and five grew to adulthood. Cora Sandlin, born December 15, 1922, died October 2, 1925, of diphtheria as she approached her third birthday. She and her sister Rose are buried in the William Roberts Cemetery in Leslie County. Rose Sandlin, the youngest child, was born May 9, 1933, and died of meningitis when she was three and a half years old.

```
DAPC-MSS-AI


Mrs. Belvia Sandlin
406 Fairlawn Road
Louisville, Kentucky  40207



Dear Mrs. Sandlin:

Reference your letter dated 2 January 1978 requesting the status of your
earlier letter of 5 August 1977.

Unfortunately, your original letter dated 5 August 1977 and the pictures
were never received by this office.

If you can possibly provide more copies of the photographs we will make
every effort to identify and provide you the history related to the
medal in question.

                                    Sincerely,



                                    WAYNE H. MORRIS
                                    Major, GS
                                    Chief, Policy and Authorizations
                                       Section
```

The Sandlins, like many rural Americans, had bad luck in dealing with our country's bureaucracies. *Sandlin Family Collection.*

Belvia lived for another fifty years after Willie died. She was active in a number of civic and community activities. *Sandlin Family Collection.*

The other five children enjoyed long, successful lives. Like their mother, they kept Willie Sandlin's memory and legacy alive.

Vorres, born April 19, 1921, went to college for one year, married and worked for Hyden Citizens Bank until her first child was born. She and her husband had four children and moved to Hamilton, Ohio in 1952. Her only son, Willie Sandlin Day, served in the Army during the Vietnam War. Vorres was a devoted wife, mother, and homemaker. She loved tending to her flower beds, cooking, and keeping a beautiful home. She was a devout Christian and an active member of the Bethel Community Church in Hamilton when she died on Christmas morning 2015 at age 94. [6]

Leona, born February 11, 1925, is still living independently as of this writing. At the age of 18 she took Vorres' place at the bank until her son was born seven years later. Leona, her husband, and son moved to Louisville in 1952. After

A HERO'S LEGACY

her divorce, she and her son lived with Belvia until 1965. Leona worked for Citizens Fidelity Bank for 38 years and retired in 1990. After dating Dr. George R. Nichols for 18 years, she married him in 1983. He died on November 19, 2001 at the age of 90.

Nancy Ruth Sandlin, born December 28, 1926, married a twin to Leona's first husband and had two children. She later divorced and married a man who was in the Navy and they had twin girls. When he was stationed overseas, Nancy and the children lived with Belvia in Louisville. In 1963 Nancy and her husband purchased a home in Louisville. After his retirement, they both became antique dealers. He died of cancer, and Nancy died in 1998 of congestive heart failure at the age of 71.

Florence, who has been a good source of information for this book, was born January 31, 1929, and was living in Winchester at the time this book was being written. At age 89, she cooks every day for her daughter and grandson who live with her, and she is an enthusiastic gardener. She is a joyful person, full of energy.

The only son, Robert E. Lee Sandlin, was born November 2, 1931. He attended pharmacy school at the University of Kentucky, passed the state exam on January 18, 1955, and later practiced his profession in Louisville. Robert E. Lee Sandlin, whose name was shortened to Bob when he entered pharmacy school bore a strong resemblance to his father. He was taller – almost 6 feet – and had his father's "dark impressive eyes." Bob joined the army after he completed his education, and while he was in the service, he married Margaret Marie Butler of Louisville in April 1956, when he was twenty-four years old. After their marriage in the third Woodland Presbyterian Church, Private Sandlin and his wife, a year his junior, moved to Arlington, Virginia, because Bob was stationed at Fort Myer. Bob was a great husband and father who was also devoted to caring for his mother's needs. Bob was a very successful pharmacist and worked tirelessly to advance his profession through state and local associations. In 1983, Sandlin, owner and operator of Colonial Drugs in St.

Matthews, was named Kentucky's Pharmacist of the Year. [7] He was humble and kindhearted and quietly did much to help people in his community, both personally and professionally. A great supporter of the University of Kentucky College of Pharmacy, he became a UK Fellow in the Fall of 2001. He loved to be outdoors, especially on the water. He was a hunter and fisherman in his younger years and later developed a love of sailing. He studied navigation, was a member of the Power Squadron, and sailed up and down both Florida coasts and to the Bahamas. He died of cancer on June 22, 2005, at the age of 73.

  Willie's children inherited the best qualities of their parents, and they have passed those values to their children. The Sandlin grandchildren, listed below, are poised to extend Willie and Belvia's legacy of honor, courage, hard work, and public responsibility well into the 21st century.

Willie and Belvia Sandlin's Children and Grandchildren

Vorres Sandlin Day & Lloyd Day
- Gloria Jean Day
- Carol Lee Deffinger
- Willie Sandlin Day
- Sherrill Lynn Bailey

Leona Sandlin Nichols
- William Dillon Asher

Nancy Sandlin Asher Brewer
- Lue Dena Peabody
- Chad Asher
- Peggy Lee Newton
- Patricia Ann Brewer

Florence Sandlin Asher Muncy
- Donna Gail Haga
- Jamie Karl Asher
- Gary Ray Asher
- Carolyn Denise Robinson
- Kim Yvette Asher
- Michelle Tina Asher

Robert E. Lee Sandlin & Margaret Butler Sandlin
- Timothy Robert Sandlin
- Phillip Douglas Sandlin

EPILOGUE

On May 1, 2018, Willie Sandlin and his wife Belvia were reinterred in the new Kentucky Veterans Cemetery South East in Hyden. More than 100 people attended this memorial ceremony, including two dozen members of Sergeant Sandlin's extended family.

"We are deeply honored to welcome SGT Willie Sandlin home to Hyden, where he raised his family and continued his service to country and community," said Commissioner Benjamin Adams of the Kentucky Department of Veterans Affairs.

Kentucky native and Vietnam Veteran Terry Hamby said that Sergeant Willie Sandlin "set the standard for soldiers for the next 100 years" and praised Sandlin for his splendid example of "humility and unassuming leadership."

Willie's daughters captured the spirit of the occasion: "My Mom and Dad loved Leslie County," said Florence. "I'm glad they are home," added Leona.

A family testimonial is presented on the following page.

May 26, 2018

Dear Dad and Mother

We know you are happy to be home and surrounded by the mountains that you loved. Even though, Florence and her family, Lue Dena and I visited you often in Zachary Taylor Cemetery in Louisville, we felt after we are gone, you would not have many visitors. We know that the people in Hyden, where you both lived most of your life, have longed for your return, and we know this is where you would prefer to be.

On Monday, April 30, 2018, you became the first residents of the Kentucky Veteran Cemetery South East. The grounds are beautiful and the mountains are breath taking. We have asked Mary Wooton to look after you. We love, miss you and think about you every day.

With our Love, Thoughts, and Prayers

Your Daughters Leona & Florence
and Your Grandchildren

My shadow was my partner in the row.
"Meeting"
Jim Wayne Miller

ACKNOWLEDGMENTS

I had only two years to complete this project, and I could not have met my deadline without the help of many people who offered both information and inspiration. I am especially grateful to John Trowbridge, Judith Kidwell, Shelby Street, and Edwina Pendarvis.

John Trowbridge is one of Kentucky's best military historians. He provided information and photographs. His military background helped me interpret and understand some of Willie's experiences.

Judith Kidwell is my administrative assistant at the JSF, and she played that role in this project, too. She took a personal interest in the project and became an expert on Sandlin's life while helping me to obtain information and photographs. She also typed this book from my hand-written manuscript. In the process, she typed/corrected more than thirty drafts before the manuscript was complete. No matter how many times I said, "Judith, can you do another round of corrections/revisions/additions," she always said, "Yes" with a smile and provided a clean manuscript by the end of the day. Judith was especially adept at keeping my footnotes straight. Over 18 months of writing, I was constantly adding new material and also re-organizing material. Judith did a masterful job of keeping the footnotes in order in spite of my constant revisions.

Shelby Street worked as my research assistant during the summer of 2017.

SERGEANT SANDLIN

He had just finished his freshman year at Columbia University, and I suspect that helping me was far less taxing than his university coursework. Shelby was ideally suited for this task by personality and experience. Shelby and his father John, the pastor of the First Methodist Church in Ashland, are both enthusiastic genealogists, and Shelby's genealogical background enabled him to gather hundreds of pieces of information that played a vital role in the completion of this book. This book would not exist without John, Judith, and Shelby.

Many organizations and individuals offered information and photographs: Stacie Petersen, The National World War I Museum & Memorial; Walter Bowman, Jennifer Patterson, Kim McDaniel, and Lisa Thompson, Kentucky Department of Libraries and Archives; Amy Purcell, Kyna Herzinger, and Marcy Werner, Archives and Special Collections, Ekstrom Library, University of Louisville; Dieter C. Ullrich, Special Collections and Archives, Camden-Carroll Library, Morehead State University; Jason Flaherty and Daniel Weddington, Margaret I. King Library, University of Kentucky; Debbie Whalen, Eastern Kentucky University Archives; Kandie Adkinson, Office of the Secretary of State; Jennifer Bartlett, University of Kentucky Libraries; Stephen Bowling, Breathitt County Public Library; Debbie Cosper, Jim Kettel, and Jim Powers, Boyd County Public Library; Clifford Hamilton and Leona Hamrick, Leslie County Public Library; Jim Stepp and Allison Holbrook, Alice Lloyd College; and the research staffs of The Library of Congress and the National Archives. James Roberts allowed the use of a photo of his grandparents, William and Sally Ann Roberts.

This book would not exist in any meaningful form without the caring assistance of my friends. For two years, Leif Clarke, Adam VanKirk, Diane Blankenship, Julianne Perry, Don Osborne, Charles and Peggy Gilley, Sharon McDonald, Caroline Wilson, Eleanor Kersey, Paula Allen, and Edwina Pendarvis listened patiently to my endless discussions of Willie Sandlin's life and accomplishments. Wayne Onkst spent a day traveling to the Breathitt County Public Library in Jackson with me, and Diane Blankenship skillfully maneuvered us through Lexington traffic for a day of research in the Margaret I. King Library at the University of Kentucky. Lew Nicholls, a retired

John Trowbridge

Edwina Pendarvis

Shelby Street

Judith Kidwell

Adam VanKirk

judge, spent several days helping me understand the complexities of Willie's Sandlin's law suit against the VFW.

Although I am responsible for the content of this book and any errors of fact and interpretation are entirely my own responsibility, I received sound advice from John Trowbridge. David L. Bettez, Kentucky's foremost historian of the Great War, former state librarian Wayne Onkst, and my long-time friend and editorial partner, Edwina Pendarvis, one of Appalachia's many fine poets, read the manuscript in its entirety and made many helpful suggestions.

Adam VanKirk lived this book with me. In 2016, he traveled with me to Florence Muncy's home in Winchester and scanned her photos and Sandlin memorabilia. Then for the next two years, he kept a file of all the photos and documents I accumulated. When my manuscript was complete, Adam paged it and designed it into the beautiful book you hold in your hands today.

I owe a debt to my office staff, particularly Laurie Cantwell and Debbie Bustetter, for tolerating my long hours of work on this project. I thank the JSF Board of Directors who encouraged me to undertake and complete this important project. Finally, I thank my friends Charles Gilley and Carl Leming and my brother Dan for their service to our country. In the process of writing about a military hero, I hope I have also honored Carl, Charles, Dan, and every other man and woman who has served in America's armed forces.

ENDNOTES

Introduction:
A Tale of Two Heroes

1. For an excellent description of Alvin York's early life, see the first two chapters of David D. Lee, *Sergeant York: An American Hero* (Lexington: The University Press of Kentucky, 1985).

2. John Perry, *Sergeant York* (Nashville: Thomas Nelson, 2010), p. viii.

3. Perry, *Sergeant York*, p. VIII. Lee, *Sergeant York*, pp. 128-130. Lee's thorough research and thoughtful writing clarifies the problems York's "hero status could create for him."

Chapter One:
Kentucky on the Eve of the Great War

1. See Thomas D. Clark's "Kentucky: A Historical Overview" in John Kleber, ed., *The Kentucky Encyclopedia* (Lexington: The University Press of Kentucky, 1992) xxvii-xxix. Hereinafter cited as KE.

2. *Ibid.*

3. David J. Bettez, *Kentucky and the Great War: World War I on the Home Front* (Lexington: The University Press of Kentucky, 2016), 49. Hereinafter cited as Bettez.

4. Bettez, 49-50.

5. Bettez, 51, 53.

6. Bettez, 62. A valuable list of the State and County Histories is provided by Bettez in his Selected Bibliography, 400-402.

7. "While Perry and Leslie County have both tried to claim this brave hero, the truth is he is and always will be a Breathitt County boy." Stephen D. Bowling, *The Jackson Times*, August 24, 2000. Hereinafter cited as Bowling. Seeking to add "local color" to Sandlin's life, some journalists reported that Sandlin lived on Devil's Jump Branch and Hell-fer-Certain Creek. Sandlin's long-time friend Joe Hart would write, in a lengthy

corrective, that "there are about as many farms on Devil's Jump as there are on the slope of the Rock of Gibraltar." *The Courier-Journal*, June 3, 1949, p. 7.

Chapter Two:
Willie Sandlin, 1890-1917

1. Not to be confused with his younger, half-brother, William Berry Sandlin, son of Willie's father John and his second wife, Lydia Bowling. Also not to be confused with his second cousin, William Eversole Sandlin.

2. In the June 5, 1900 Census, Willie's mother was living in Wooten, Leslie County, Kentucky. She was head of household, declared a widow, and raising six children alone. In the June 11, 1900 Census, Willie's father was in the Kentucky State Penitentiary.

3. Stephen D. Bowling to JMG, personal interview in Jackson, Kentucky, September 7, 2017. Mr. Bowling, in addition to being an accomplished local historian, is the Director of the Breathitt County Public Library and actively involved in the intellectual and political life of his community.

4. Harlan County Court Orders, April 11 – April 29, 1989, pp. 465-508, Register of Convicts, Kentucky Penitentiary; Harlan County, Prisoner Register, 1898, p. 155.

5. *Richmond Daily Register*, October 3, 1919; *Greencastle* (IN) *Herald*, December 12, 1924, Berry Craig, *Hidden History of Kentucky Soldiers* (The History Press, Arcadia Publishing, 2011), pp. 69-71.

6. *Richmond Daily Register*, October 3, 1919.

7. *The Courier-Journal*, September 2, 1941, p. 7. Alvin York was also a fighter when he was a boy. As a young man, he was six feet tall and weighed 175 pounds. He "had acquired the nickname 'Big 'un' and insisted he was never once beaten or knocked down by an opponent." Lee, *Sergeant York*, pp. 6-7.

8. "Kentucky Did Not Forget Willie Sandlin, World War I Hero," *The Kentucky Explorer*, September, 1993, p. 45.

9. "Anti-German Hysteria in World War I Kentucky," *Northern Kentucky Heritage*, Vol. XV, No. 1, p. 10.

10. KE, p. 433; quoted in Bettez, p. 30; *The Courier-Journal*, June 5, 1918.

11. First Sergeant Vance H. Marchbanks quoted in "Buffalo Soldiers at Huachuca: 10th Cavalry Contributions to the Punitive Expedition," p. 4.

ENDNOTES

12. For more information, see *Huachuca Illustrated: A Magazine of the Fort Huachuca Museum*, Vol. 2, 1999.

13. Edward L.N. Glass, *The History of the Tenth Cavalry: 1866-1921*, p. 83. In his history of the 10th Cavalry, Edward Glass recalls the importance of intelligence on German activities in Mexico.

> About August 15, 1918, the Intelligence Division reported the presence of strange Mexicans, plentifully supplied with arms, ammunition, food and clothing, gathering in increasing numbers in and about Nogales, Sonora; also the presence of several strange white men, apparently Germans, at times engaged in addressing gatherings of Mexicans explaining military terms, movements and methods. At about this time an anonymous letter was received, written by a person who claimed to have been a major in Villa's forces who was sickened and disgusted at the atrocities committed by Villa and his men, and at the lack of pay or reward, and who claimed a feeling of friendly respect for American troops, warning them of the German influences at work near and in Nogales, advising of the financial activities of the German agents, and of a contemplated attack on Nogales about August 25, 1918. This letter rang so true that it became a subject of investigation by Lieutenant Colonel Frederick J. Herman, 10th Cavalry, then action sub district commander at Nogales, and Lieutenant Robert Scott Israel, Infantry Intelligence Officer at Nogales, and so many points of the letter were verified that it was given more than ordinary weight.

14. *The Courier-Journal*, September 2, 1941, p. 7.

15. *The Courier-Journal*, June 3, 1949, p. 7.

16. Howard Park to his grandmother, Mrs. Addie Parker, Fort Scott (KS) *Daily Tribune*, June 7, 1918, p.2.

17. *The Public Ledger* (Maysville, KY), October 22, 1921, Afternoon Edition; Jim Webb, *Born Fighting*, p. 255.

Chapter Three:
Willie Receives the Medal of Honor

1. *Lexington Herald*, September 18, 1919.

SERGEANT SANDLIN

2. Arthur Beverly to a relative in Maple Park, Illinois, *The Daily Chronicle* (DeKalb, IL) August 5, 1918, p.1. Beverly had written the letter from the trenches "with my gas mask for a desk" and he hoped "the letter proved better than the desk."

3. For more information, see Douglas V. Mastriano, *Thunder in the Argonne: A New History of America's Greatest Battle* (Lexington: The University Press of Kentucky, 2017.) Mastriano offers the most comprehensive account of the legendary campaign to date. Mastriano is also the author of *Alvin York: A New Biography of the Hero of the Argonne*, also published by the University Press of Kentucky.

4. Lieutenant T. H. Embry to his uncle G. W. Embry, *The Courier-Journal,* September 13, 1918, p. 12.

5. John C. Super, ed., *The United States at War*, Vol. 1 (Pasadena: Salem Press, Inc., 2005), pp. 360-364.

6. *The Lexington Leader*, July 22, 1929, pp. 1-2.

7. *Richmond Daily Register*, October 3, 1919; Mary Breckinridge, *Wide Neighborhoods: A Story of the Frontier Nursing Service* (Lexington: The University Press of Kentucky, 1952), p. 173; Neace, *Kentucky Explorer*, pp. 54-60; Caldwell, "Above and Beyond," p. 10; *Perry Hazard Herald*, July 24, 1919; *The Courier-Journal*, July 21, 1919, p. 3.

8. The Library of Congress, John J. Pershing Papers: Diaries, Notebooks, and Address Books, 1882-1925; Diaries; Set 1: 1918, Sept. 2 – 1919, Jan. 27.

9. *Tyrone* (PA) *Daily Herald*, December 11, 1924; "Kentucky Did Not Forget Willie Sandlin, World War I Hero," *The Kentucky Explorer*, September, 1993, p. 46; *Lexington Leader*, September 1, 1919; *The Courier-Journal*, July 21, 1919, p. 3.

10. Fred P. Caldwell, "Above and Beyond the Call of Duty," *Register of Kentucky State Historical Society*, Vol. 18, No. 53 (May, 1920), p. 9; *The Courier-Journal*, July 21, 1919, p. 3.

11. *New York Times*, February 2, 1919, p. 8.

12. *Richmond Daily Register*, October 3, 1919; *The Courier-Journal*, July 21, 1919, p. 3.

13. Florence Muncy to JMG. His discharge showed that he was involved in the following battles: Meuse-Argonne, 9-16-18 and 10-11-18; Bois de Forge 9-26-18; Occupation of Vaden Lines, 6-23-18 and 8-23-18; Amiens Sector, Hamel, 7-4-18; St. Hilaire Marchville, Bois de Warfield, Bois de Harville, 11-10-18; Army of Occupation 12-7-18 to 4-26-19.

ENDNOTES

14. Craig, *Hidden History of Kentucky Soldiers*, pp. 69-71; James Clell Neace, "Recalling Sergeant Willie Sandlin, World War I Hero From Kentucky," *The Kentucky Explorer*, September, 1988, p. 59; "Wonderful Exploits of Sergt. Willie Sandlin," *Perry Hazard Herald*, Thursday, July 24, 1919; *The Courier-Journal*, July 21, 1919, p. 3. By the summer of 1919, Kentucky newspapers were announcing that Sandlin had "returned to his home in Leslie County." *The Courier-Journal,* July 13, 1919, p. 8.

15. "Hero Willie Sandlin Takes Freedom to His Brother Charles," *The Courier-Journal*, November 13, 1919; "Governor Black Parsons Hero Sandlin's Brother," *Richmond Daily Register*, November 13, 1919, p. 1; *The* (Danville) *Advocate Messenger*, July 28, 1931, p. 2; *The Courier-Journal*, July 28, 1931, p. 2.

16. *The Lexington Leader*, December 9, 1919, p. 1.

17. "Slayer of 24 Germans Escort for War Dead," *The Washington Times*, December 21, 1919, pp. 2-3; *Tyrone* (PA) *Daily Herald*, December 11, 1924; *Ft. Wayne* (IN) *Sentinel*, December 20, 1919; Mary South, a Sandlin cousin, in an Ancestry.com post on November 7, 2009; *The Courier-Journal*, January 10, 1920, p. 3; The Junction City (KS) *Daily Union*, February 13, 1920, p. 7.

18. *The Courier-Journal,* May 29, 1920, p. 3; The Lexington *Herald*, May 29, 1920, p. 1; *The Lexington Leader*, December 9, 1919, p. 1.

19. *Ibid.*

Chapter Four:
Marriage, Early Family Life and the Community

1. FM to JMG; *Tyrone* (PA) *Daily Herald*, December 11, 1924.

2. "The Sitting Down Job," *The Courier-Journal*, June 3, 1920; *Ibid*, "Bandit Shot In Liquor Battle," October 31, 1920, p. 1; *Ibid*, "Distillery Guard Fires At 3 Youths," April 26, 1921, p. 4; "Distillery Guards Drive Bandits Off, *The Courier-Journal*, November 158, 1921, p. 1; "Move [sic] Men Held in Huffacker Murder," *Ibid,* February 23, 1923, p. 1. This article indicated that seven men were being held in the Lexington jail for the murder of a guard at Old Joe Distillery.

3. "Guard at Distillery," *Richmond Daily Register*, August 5, 1922, p. 1; *The Courier-Journal*, August 12, 1922, p. 6; *Richmond Daily Register*, December 4, 1922, p. 1; "Too Tame For Warrior," *The Lexington Leader*, November 13, 1922, p. 4.

4. Florence Muncy to JMG.

5. "The Restless Decade," by Bruce Catton. *American Heritage, Special Issue: The 1920s*, Vol. VXI, No. 5 (American Heritage Publishing Company: New York, NY, 1965), pp. 5-6.

6. *Thousandsticks*, September 22, 1922.

5. Lexington *Herald*, September 2, 1919; *Ibid.*, August 31, 1919.

6. *Tyrone* (PA) *Daily Herald*, December 11, 1924; *Richmond Daily Register*, September 7, 1921; *Mt. Sterling Advocate*, August 22, 1922; *Greencastle* (IN) *Herald*, December 12, 1924; *The* (Shreveport) *Times*, September 7, 1924, p. 11; *The Greenwood* (MS) *Commonwealth*, December 15, 1924, p. 5; "Pershing Is To Review Parade," The Bridgewater (NJ) *Courier-News*, August 13, 1924, p.4.

7. *The Courier-Journal*, August 29, 1925, p. 18; *Ibid.*, January 17, 1926, p. 10.

8. "Slayer of Vet Given 4 Years," *The Courier-Journal*, June 27, 1928, p. 1.

9. *The Courier-Journal*, June 14, 1927, p. 16; *Ibid.*, May 8, 1947, p. 14; *Ibid*, June 23, 1928, p. 2; *The Orlando* (FL) *Sentinel*, September 30, 1929, p. 1; *The Courier-Journal*, September 30, 1929, pp. 1-2.

10. Sam K. Cowan, *Sergeant York and His People* (New York: Grosset & Dunlap, 1922), p. 276. Willie named his son for Robert E. Lee Murphy, a Lexington attorney who served with Willie in France. FM to JMG, February 22, 2017.

11. Florence Muncy to JMG.

Chapter Five:
Improving His Eastern Kentucky Homeland

1. Brewer, *Rugged Trail to Appalachia*, p. 35.

2. Breckinridge, *Wide Neighborhoods*, p. 173.

3. *The Courier-Journal*, June 27, 1928, p. 1 and 3.

4. "State's Greatest War Hero Will Help Stamp Out Illiteracy in Mountains," *Lexington Herald-Leader*, September 7, 1919, p. 8.

5. "Crusader to Wipe Out All Illiteracy in United States by 1930," *The Gettysburg* (PA) *Times*, April 26, 1926, p. 2; "Recalling Willie Sandlin," Letter to the Editor by Malcolm H. Holliday, Jr. in *The Kentucky Explorer*, November 1993, p. 4. FM and Leona Nichols to JMG.

6. Yvonne Honeycutt Baldwin, *Cora Wilson Stewart and Kentucky's Moonlight*

ENDNOTES

Schools (Lexington: The University Press of Kentucky, 2006), pp. 113-114. See also "Boyce is Best School Taught by Moonlight," *Louisville Courier-Journal*, October 23, 1919' *Lexington Herald*, October 4, 1919; *Ibid.*, September 28, 1919.

7. "Campbell Will Take Challenge of Robertson," *The Courier-Journal,* September 29, 1919, p. 3; *Lexington Herald*, November 2, 1919.

8. *Herald-Leader*, November 2, 1919. Letter of May 14, 1921, from Legation to Mr. Willie Sandlin in general file of the Cora Wilson Stewart Papers at the Margaret I. King Library, University of Kentucky.

9. "Kentucky Hero Will Make Plea For Education," Leslie County *Thousandsticks*, September 18, 1919.

10. Cora Wilson Stewart, *Moonlight Schools* (New York: E. P. Sutton & Company, 1922) p. 107. The author owns a First Edition signed "To Bun and Mary From Cora, Christmas, 1923."

11. Louisville *Courier-Journal*, April 20, 1942; see also Lee, *Sergeant York*, p. 117.

12. Florence Muncy to JMG; newspaper articles in the 1920s and 1930s regularly brought attention to the fact that Sandlin "while not in destitute circumstances [was] barely able to eke out a meager existence for himself" and his family. *The Lexington Herald*, December 30, 1925, p. 12.

Chapter Six:
No Veterans Benefits for a Wounded Hero, 1921-1933

1. *The Courier-Journal*, March 12, 1925; *Ibid*, July 21, 1919.

2. FM to JMG, February 22, 2017.

3. "Congressional Medal Soldier Welcome," *The Chillicothe* (MO) *Constitution*, February 27, 1928.

4. *Ibid.*

5. *Ibid.*

6. There is a large – and ever growing – body of secondary literature on chemical warfare during World War I. See, for example, Gerald J. Fitzgerald, "Chemical Warfare and Medical Response During World War I," *American Journal of Public Health*, July 2008; Sheryl Ubelacher, "How First World War medical advances still benefit patients today," *The Canadian Press*, September 2, 2014; Ellen Hampton, "How World War I Revolutionized Medicine," *The Atlantic*, February 24, 2017; Chemical Weapons

in World War I," *Wikipedia*.

7. *New York Tribune*, October 23, 1921, p. 10; *The Public Ledger* (Maysville, KY), October 22, 1921, Afternoon Edition. *Richmond Daily Register,* October 19, 1921, p. 1; The (Maysville) *Public Ledger*, October 22, 1921, p. 1; *The Lexington Herald*, October 21, 1921, reported that "Sergeant Sandlin had a severe affection [affliction] of the lungs . . ."

8. *The Lexington Herald*, October 21, 1921.

9. Greencastle (IN) *Herald*, December 12, 1924; "Kentucky Did Not Forget Willie Sandlin, World War I Hero", *The Kentucky Explorer*, September, 1993, p. 45.

10. *The Courier-Journal*, January 5, 1925, p. 2; *Ibid*, March 12, 1925, p. 5.

11. See Murphy's obituary in the *Lexington Herald-Leader*, April 6, 1968. Like many of his WWI comrades, Murphy lived a long life after the war. He died on April 5, 1968, one day after Martin Luther King had been assassinated in Memphis, Tennessee.

12. "Hero Keeps to Mountain Home," *The Circleville* (OH) *Herald*, January 5, 1925, p. 5.

13. *The Courier-Journal,* October 22, 1925, p. 3.

14. *The Courier-Journal*, December 8, 1925, p. 4.

15. *The Courier-Journal*, January 23, 1926, p. 11.

16. "Governor to Aid in Hero Drive," *The Courier-Journal,* January 3, 1926, p. 11; *Ibid.*, January 28, 1926, p. 20; *Ibid.*, January 29, 1926, p. 4.

17. *The Courier-Journal,* February 10, 1926, p. 22.

18. *The Courier-Journal*, February 17, 1926, p. 8; *Ibid,* February 11, 1926, p. 4.

19. *The Courier-Journal,* March 26, 1926, p. 4.

20. "Murphy Flayed in House Report," *The Courier-Journal*, March 16, 1926, p. 1.

21. "Want Compensation of Sandlin Reinstated," *The Lexington Leader*, May 18, 1927, p. 11.

22. "Disabled Vets End Convention," *The Courier-Journal*, June 14, 1927, p. 16.

23. "Foreign War Vets End Encampment," *The Courier-Journal*, June 27, 1927, p. 3.

24. *The Chillicothe* (MO) *Constitution-Tribune*, February 27, 1928, p. 4.

25. *The* (Danville, Kentucky) *Advocate-Messenger*, October 11, 1928, p. 2. *Ibid.*, October 13, 1928, p. 1; *The* (Helena, MT) *Independent Record*, December 20, 1928, p. 8.

ENDNOTES

26. "World War Vets Converge Today on Louisville, KY," *The Oshkosh* (WI) *Northwestern*, September 28, 1929, p. 6; "Sergeant Sandlin Gets His Uniform," *The Courier-Journal*, September 28, 1929, p. 3; *The Scranton* (PA) *Republican*, October 1, 1929, p. 22.

27. *The Courier-Journal,* March 12, 1925, p. 5; *Ibid.,* February 16, 1928, p. 2; *The Indianapolis Star,* April 17, 1928, p. 11; *The Chillicothe* (MO) *Constitution-Tribune*, February 27, 1928, p. 4.

28. "He Loved the Game of Politics," *The Courier-Journal*, March 29, 1963, p. 8; Ibid., March 22, 1963, p. 14; *Ibid.*, July 11, 1917, p. 2.

29. *The Chillicothe* (MO) *Constitution-Tribune*, February 27, 1928, p. 4.

30. "War Vets Name Fowler Head," *The Courier-Journal*, July 1, 1928, p. 4. See also *The Cincinnati Enquirer-Kentucky Edition*, January 25, 1928, p. 1 for more information on Senator Hiram Brock's attempts to pass a bill into law that would provide funds for Sandlin who was living "in a two-room cabin in the mountains, 18 miles from a railroad."

31. *The Encyclopedia of Southern Culture,* Vol. 3, p. 110; *The Courier Journal*, October 22, 1929, p. 9.

32. Trevor Hammond, July 1, 2017. https//blog.newspapers.com/bonus-army-forced-from-the-capital-july-28-1932; Maurice Matloff, editor, *American Military History*, Vol. 2: 1902-1996 (Combined Books, Inc: Conshocken, PA, 1996), pp. 70-71.

33. *The Encyclopedia of Southern Culture*, Vol. 3, p. 110; *The Courier-Journal*, October 22, 1929, p. 9.

Chapter Seven:
Financial Distress, Hard Times, and Health Problems During the Depression

1. "Hero Says He Has Not Become Tobacco Planter," *The Lexington Herald*, March 12, 1925, p. 9.

2. Florence Muncy to JMG, June 7, 2017.

3. Belvia Sandlin to CWS, September 27, 1925; *Ibid.*, October 8, 1925; *Ibid.*, June 17, 1932; Belvia Sandlin to CWS, July 25, 1932; *Ibid.*, September 8, 1932; *Ibid.*, October 29, 1932.

4. Mary T. Brewer, *Rugged Trail to Appalachia: A History of Leslie County, Kentucky and Its People Celebrating Its Centennial Year, 1878-1978*. (Viper, Kentucky, Graphic

SERGEANT SANDLIN

Arts Press, 1978), p. 13.

5. Mary T. Brewer, who taught in the Leslie County schools for a decade, did an excellent job of assembling Leslie County superstitions and folk practices in her book *Rugged Trail to Appalachia* (Viper, Kentucky: Graphic Arts Press, 1978), see especially pages 25 and 26.

6. Belvia Sandlin to Cora Wilson Stewart, June 17, 1932; *Ibid*, July 25, 1932; *Ibid*; September 8, 1932; Cora Wilson Stewart to Belvia Sandlin, September 12, 1932.

7. More than 100 interviews with Willie Sandlin's daughter Florence provided this material on the Sandlins as subsistence farmers. Florence was eighty-eight years old at the time of these personal visits and telephone interviews, but she had a very clear memory of her childhood on the farm on Owl's Nest Creek, a half mile from Hyden.

8. Brewer, *Rugged Trail to Appalachia*, p. 19.

9. Earl Hamner, Jr., *The Homecoming* (New York: Avon Books, 1970), pp. 31-32.

Chapter Eight:
Hyden

1. Brewer, *Rugged Trail to Appalachia*, p. 3.

2. "Leslie Gets First Road," *Louisville Courier-Journal*, August 20, 1922.

3. *Thousandsticks*, April 27, 1911. *Ibid.*, May 11, 1911.

4. In the 1950s, Willie's daughter Florence and her husband ran a theatre, a restaurant, and a skating rink in Hyden.

5. "Backwoods Kentucky Listens In," by Frances Jewell McVey. *Forum and Century* (1930-1940) July 1934, pp. 51-53.

Chapter Nine:
Still Trying for Financial Assistance in the 1930s

1. *The Courier-Journal*, January 28, 1926, p. 20. Sandlin was determined not to commercialize his war experiences. In an announcement of his death, a Lexington newspaper reported that "only recently, he declined to permit his life story to be written for motion picture use." *The Lexington Herald*, May 30, 1949, p. 8. Also see *The Lexington Leader*, January 29, 1926, p. 7.

2. Belvia Sandlin to Cora Wilson Stewart, from Hyden, KY Box 36, June 17, 1932;

ENDNOTES

Ibid, July 25, 1932.

3. Cora Wilson Stewart to Mrs. Will Sandlin, September 2, 1932.

4. Belvia Sandlin to Cora Wilson Stewart, September 8, 1932.

5. Cora Wilson Stewart to Belvia Sandlin, September 12, 1932.

6. Herman H. Fox to Robert E. Lee Murphy, October 22, 1932. A copy of this letter was sent to the Sandlins and Belvia hand-copied it for Cora Wilson Stewart.

7. Cora Wilson Stewart to Belvia Sandlin, November 2, 1932.

8. Herman H. Fox to Robert E. Lee Murphy, October 22, 1932.

9. *Ibid.*

10. Plaintiff's reply to Michael B. Gilligan, George Freeman, and John Sweikel, June 3, 1935. Willie Sandlin vs. VFW. Leslie County, Kentucky.

11. *Ibid.*

12. G. Richardson, *Banking Panics of 1930-1931*. Retrieved from Federal Reserve History: htts//www.federalreservehistory.org/essays/banking_panics_1930_31, *passim*.

13. Settlement and Orders of the Courts, April 23, 1937. Leslie County, Kentucky.

14. This situation exemplified the difficulties in writing a biography of Willie Sandlin. Historians are limited when facts are limited. Sandlin left no personal records, so the judgment that he never received money from the Hero Fund was based on "Willie told that to Belvia, and Belvia told that to Florence."

15. *The Courier-Journal,* January 28, 1930, p. 3; *The Bismark* (ND) *Tribune*, January 2, 1930, p 6. See also *Sioux Falls* (SD) *Argus-Leader*, May 14, 1930, p. 2, and *The Lincoln* (NE) *Star*, May 14, 1930, p. 9.

16. Morgan, "War Hero Dies," *The Jackson Times*; *The Lexington Leader*, March 29, 1932, p. 4.

17. N. E. Whiting, Adjudication Officer, Veterans Administration to Willie Sandlin, June 7, 1933.

18. Discharge Certificate, Veterans Administration Diagnostic Center, Hines, Illinois, December 30, 1935.

19. "Vet Votes to Enlist If U.S. Enters Strife," *The Lexington Leader*, September 8, 1939, p. 10.

20. *The Courier-Journal,* August 25, 1940, p. 36; *Ibid.*, April 13, 1941, p. 63.

SERGEANT SANDLIN

21. "Hero of World War I Plans to Move Here." *The Lexington Leader*, July 30, 1942, p. 1.

22. David D. Lee, *Sergeant York: An American Hero* (Lexington: The University Press of Kentucky, 1985), pp. 116-117.

23. *Thousandsticks*, December 11, 1941.

Chapter Ten:
The 1940s – A War's Hero Death

1. *Thousandsticks,* December 25, 1941.

2. "Hero Prefers the Hills," *Pittsburgh* (PA) *Post-Gazette*, December 24, 1941, p. 21.

3. Interview with Amerdia "Merdie" Morris by Stephen D. Bowling, September 1996.

4. Florence Muncy to JMG, July 27, 2017; *Ibid.,* June 7, 2017.

5. United States of America, Certificate of Award, Office of Price Administration, 3 July, 1944.

6. *Thousandsticks*, June 2, 1949; *The Courier-Journal*, October 10, 1932, p. 4.

7. Letter to the Editor from Ray Huff, *The Courier-Journal*, November 4, 1941, p. 6.

8. *Thousandsticks*, November 6, 1941.

9. "Commission Urged For Willie Sandlin," *The Courier-Journal,* May 21, 1942, p. 14.

10. Death Record, Form V.S. 1-A, State File No. 12197, Registrar's No. 2582, R. D. Metheny, M.D. Chief Professional Services.

11. "Leslie County Pays Last Tribute to its World War I Hero," *Thousandsticks*, June 2, 1949.

12. "A Hero Dies," *The Lexington Leader*, May 31, 1949, p. 4.

Chapter Eleven:
A Hero's Legacy

1. Florence Muncy to JMG, July 27, 2017; *Thousandsticks*, June 2, 1949.

2. "Kentucky's Congressional Medal of Honor Winner Reinterred at Zachary Taylor National Cemetery," *The Kentucky Legionnaire*, October 1990, 9.

3. Craig, *Hidden History of Kentucky Soldiers*, pp. 69-71; *Frontier Nursing Service Quarterly Bulletin*, Vol. 51, No. 2, Autumn 1975, p. 43; Lexington *Herald-Leader*, July

ENDNOTES

30, 2008; "Beshear Unveils Medal of Honor Plaque," Kentucky Press News Service, March 15, 2012.

4. "Sandlin Widow Presented New Ribbon For Medal," *Courier-Journal*, May 21, 1983.

5. *The Courier-Journal,* February 6, 1999, p. 10; Owen Morgan, "Wife of Leslie County War Hero Dies," *The Jackson Times*; *Leslie County News*, February 11, 1999.

6. Vorres' marriage to William Lloyd Day was announced in the *Quarterly Bulletin of the Frontier Nursing Service, Inc.*, Vol. 18, No. 3, Winter 1943.

7. Florence Muncy to JMG.

8. *The Courier-Journal*, September 18, 1998, p. 16.

8. "Son of Medal Winner Prefers Pharmacy Career," *The Courier-Journal*, June 6, 1954, p. 22; *The Courier-Journal,* January 18, 1955, p. 28; *Ibid,* April 21, 1956, p. 27; *Ibid.*, May 12, 1956, p. 16; *The Courier-Journal,* September 12, 1983; *Ibid*, June 14, 2015, p. 87.

General John J. Pershing at the White House, Armistice Day, 1938. Fifty years after Pershing presented the Medal of Honor to Willie Sandlin, hardened old veterans of the Great War still toasted "Black Jack Pershing" and spoke his name with reverence.
Library of Congress, Prints & Photographs Division, photograph by Harris & Ewing.

CHRONOLOGY

1885 | John "Dirty Face" Sandlin and Lucinda Abner marry.

January 1, 1890 | Willie Sandlin born on Long's Creek in Breathitt County to John "Dirty Face" Sandlin and Lucinda Abner Sandlin. He is the second of five children.

1900 | John and Lucinda Sandlin divorce.

1900 | John Sandlin is jailed for murder, leaves Kentucky when released.

August 8, 1900 | Lucinda Abner Sandlin dies in childbirth in Breathitt County.

1900 | Willie and his brothers are divided among relatives. Willie goes to live with his father's relatives on Hell For Certain Creek in Leslie County.

April 16, 1913 | Sandlin enlists in the regular army in Jackson, Breathitt County.

July, 1916 | Company H of 35th Infantry organized at Nogales, Arizona. Corporal Willie Sandlin is a member.

April 6, 1917 | United States declares war on Germany,

April 16, 1917 | Willie's enlistment expires while he is stationed in Nogales. He re-enlists the next day, and he is assigned to 132nd Infantry, 33rd Division.

June, 1917 | Willie is sent to Europe as part of General Pershing's American Expeditionary Force.

1918 | Sandlin promoted to Sergeant in Company A, 132nd Infantry, 33rd Division.

September 26 - November 11, 1918 | Meuse-Argonne Offensive

September 26, 1918 | In battle at Bois de Forges, France, Sandlin destroys three German machine gun nests and kills twenty-four enemy combatants; for these acts of valor, he is recommended to receive the Medal of Honor.

October 9, 1918 | Sandlin is gassed in the Argonne Forest fighting, refuses medical attention.

November 11, 1918 | The Armistice is signed and the war ends.

SERGEANT SANDLIN

February, 1919 | Sandlin receives his Medal of Honor from General Pershing at Chaumont, France, the general headquarters of the American Expeditionary Forces.

May 30, 1919 | Willie is discharged from the army at Camp Grant in Rockford, Illinois. Willie returns to Leslie county.

Fall, 1919 | Willie tours Kentucky with Cora Wilson Stewart, founder of the Moonlight Schools, to advocate for literacy in rural areas and the value of education.

December, 1919 | On account of his exemplary record, Willie is appointed special escort for the bodies of soldiers who had died overseas. He leaves again for France the following month.

June 4, 1920 | Sandlin returns to Eastern Kentucky and marries Belvia Roberts in Hyden. They live on William Robert's property in the "weaning house." William later loans Willie the money to purchase a small farm with a house on the property.

April 19, 1921 | Willie and Belvia's first daughter, Vorres Sandlin, is born.

1921 | Willie begins working as distillery guard in Leslie County. He is laid off due to lack of funds in December 1922.

October - November, 1921 | Sandlin is one of twenty-five Medal of Honor recipients to attend American Legion convention in Kansas City, Missouri. He continues to attend state and national meetings of the American Legion and the Veterans of Foreign Wars (VFW).

October, 1921 | Willie is examined in Richmond, Kentucky, and is reported as suffering from a lung infection as a result of gas inhaled during the war.

December 15, 1922 | Willie and Belvia's second daughter, Cora Wilson Stewart Sandlin, is born. She dies of childhood diseases three years later.

1923 | Willie's army benefits are cut from $40 to just $10 per month.

1924 | Willie attends the VFW encampment in Atlantic City. Along with other Medal of Honor recipients, he calls on President Coolidge and serves as General Pershing's aide in the proceedings.

February 11, 1925 | Willie and Belvia's third daughter, Leona Sandlin, is born.

December, 1925 | Mary Breckinridge founds the Frontier Nursing Service in Leslie County. Willie and Belvia become volunteers.

CHRONOLOGY

December 28, 1926 | Willie and Belvia's fourth daughter, Nancy Ruth Sandlin, is born.

1926 | VFW establishes the "Hero Fund" for Willie Sandlin's relief.

June 16, 1928 | Hyden Hospital of Frontier Nursing Service is dedicated.

September, 1928 | While Willie is attending the VFW encampment in Denver, his brother Elihu is shot and killed in Leslie County.

January 31, 1929 | Willie and Belvia's fifth daughter, Florence Norwood Sandlin, is born and delivered by Frontier Nursing Service nurse-midwives.

September, 1929 | 50,000 veterans, including Willie, attend the VFW encampment in Louisville, Kentucky. Despite Willie's efforts and the support of veterans' organizations, compensation for his injuries is not forthcoming.

1930s | Faced with the hardship of the Great Depression, the Sandlins turn to subsistence farming. Willie works for much of the Depression at a WPA road-building job.

November 2, 1932 | Willie and Belvia's first and only son, Robert E. Lee Sandlin, is born.

1932 - 1937 | Willie Sandlin pursues his "Hero Fund" money through legal action, to no apparent avail.

May 9, 1933 | Willie and Belvia's sixth daughter and last child, Rose Sandlin, is born. She dies four years later of childhood diseases.

September, 1940 | The first peacetime draft in American history is signed in preparation for possible war. Willie Sandlin registers despite being 52 years old and not required to participate in the draft.

December, 1941 | William Roberts, Belvia's father, dies and the Sandlins inherit one third of his large property. They later purchase another third of the land from Belvia's brother, Watt.

1941 | Willie seeks political office as Leslie County jailer, but falls short of winning the seat.

May 29, 1949 | Willie Sandlin dies in the V.A. Hospital in Louisville, Kentucky, at the age of 59. He is buried with full military honors in Hurricane Cemetery in Hyden.

June, 5 1964 | Kentucky Highway Historical Marker No. 631, honoring Sergeant Willie

SERGEANT SANDLIN

Sandlin, is installed on the courthouse grounds at Hyden, Leslie County, Kentucky.

September 27, 1975 | Dedication of Sergeant Willie Sandlin Memorial U. S. Army Reserve Training Center, Hyden, Leslie County, Kentucky.

September 27, 1975 | Recognition of Sandlin's life by Hyden Lodge No. 664 F. & A.M. He is honored as a leader and for his valuable service to his Lodge and the Masonic Fraternity.

August 14, 1976 | Dedication of Kentucky Obelisk, Medal of Honor Grove, Freedom Foundation, Valley Forge, Pennsylvania. Belvia attends the ceremony.

September, 1990 | Reinterment from Hurricane Cemetery near Hyden, Kentucky to Zachary Taylor National Cemetery in Louisville, Kentucky, with the ceremonial assistance of the American Legion.

September 19, 1998 | Nancy Ruth Sandlin Brewer dies in Louisville, Kentucky, at age 71.

February 5, 1999 | Belvia Roberts Sandlin dies in Louisville, Kentucky, at age 96. She is buried next to Willie.

May 28, 1999 | Dedication of National Medal of Honor Memorial, Indianapolis, Marion County, Indiana.

November 12, 2001 | Dedication of Kentucky Medal of Honor Memorial, Louisville, Jefferson County, Kentucky.

June 22, 2005 | Robert E. Lee Sandlin dies of cancer in Louisville, Kentucky, at age 73, after a successful career as a pharmacist.

December 25, 2015 | Vorres Sandlin Day dies in Hamilton, Ohio, at age 94.

June 24, 2016 | Dedication of "Sergeant Willie Sandlin Memorial Bridge" on Kentucky Route 30, near the intersection of Kentucky Route 3237 in Breathitt County.

APPENDIX A

Additional Information Concerning Sandlin's Medals

U.S. Decorations

The Medal of Honor, first established as the Naval Medal of Valor, now called the Medal of Honor, in 1861 and the Army Medal of Honor in 1862, is the highest American military decoration. It is usually bestowed personally in the name of Congress by the President of the United States in Washington D.C. to the recipient or their next of kin. There have been 3515 Medals of Honor awarded for "Conspicuous gallantry and intrepidity at the risk of life above and beyond the call of duty" since the distinction was established, almost half of which were given for service in the Civil War. The Army Medal of Honor is a five-pointed gold star featuring Minerva's head surrounded by the words "United States of America". The recipient's name is also engraved on the award following the words "The Congress to."

The Purple Heart, first awarded in 1932, is awarded on behalf of the President to any soldier who has sustained an injury on or after April 5, 1917, while serving the U.S. Military. It is the successor to the Badge of Military Merit, which was simply a heart-shaped, purple cloth established by George Washington in 1782 and only awarded to three soldiers. The award was revived on the 200th anniversary of Washington's birth by executive order of the President to be first awarded to General Douglas MacArthur. During the early years of the award, especially at the beginning of the Second World War, the Purple Heart was awarded not only for wounds, but for meritorious service. Anyone with a Certificate of Merit, such as Willie's signed by Pershing, could turn it in for a Purple Heart. After 1943, however, the Purple Heart was restricted to those with wounds exclusively. Over the years, it has been expanded to include posthumous awarding and awards to those who sustained wounds during terrorist attacks or as part of a peacekeeping force. A profile portrait of George Washington adorns the heart, which hangs from a purple ribbon.

The Legion of Merit, established in 1942, is awarded for exceptionally meritorious service. It is now almost solely awarded to high-ranking military officials, generals, and admirals. However, from 1942 through 1944, it was the only award for valor in combat below the Silver Star, so it was awarded to the lower ranks for a wider variety of achievements. It can also be awarded to military or political representatives of foreign governments. The Legion of Merit is unique in that it is the only U.S decoration besides the Medal of Honor to be worn around the neck and is the only U.S. decoration to be awarded in degrees, somewhat like an order of Chivalry. The first Legion of Merit was awarded to Amaro Soares Bittencourt, a Brigadier General in the Brazilian Army, in October 1942. The second Legion of Merit, awarded a week later, was the first to be awarded to a U.S. service member, Lieutenant Junior Grade Ann A. Bernatitus, a Navy nurse, for her service in the defense of the Philippines. The medal has a white, five-point star design, with V-shaped cuts into the end of each point of the star, which is lined with a dark red. In the center is a navy blue background with white stars, making the entire medal resemble the U.S flag. This design sits atop a gold medal which is surrounded by a green wreath.

The Bronze Star, established in 1944, was conceived as a way to improve soldier's morale by allowing Captains in the forces to have an award to bestow upon those under their command who had performed heroic or meritorious acts in a combat zone. When it is awarded for valor in combat, the Combat V is worn on the medal. The medal can also be awarded to civilians serving alongside U.S. forces in combat situations, such as in the case of Joe Galloway, a reporter who rescued a badly wounded soldier in combat in Vietnam. The Bronze Star is awarded for acts that are not deemed extraordinary enough for a Silver Star or a Legion of Merit but are still distinct from the expected duties of the combatant. It ranks just above the Purple Heart in precedence. As the name implies, it is a bronze star hung from a red ribbon with a blue stripe lined in white running vertically down the middle. On the back of the medal, an inscription reads, "Heroic or Meritorious Achievement" with the engraved name of the recipient.

The U.S Army Marksmanship Badge, a qualification established in 1881 with the U.S. Army's Marksman Button, is an award now given to soldiers who perform well in Qualifications Courses with their weapon. It comes in three different ranks: the highest, expert, like Willie's, and then sharpshooter and marksman. There is a badge awarded for each type of weapon proficiency. The badges are awarded to both officers and soldiers, with the enlisted soldiers and non-commissioned officers expected, as a part of army tradition, to display them on their uniforms. These badges are also sometimes awarded to civilians by the Civilian Marksmanship Program of the Corporation for the Promotion of Rifle Practice and Firearm Safety. Sandlin received this honor in 1916, before he shipped off to France, so it was likely for excellence in training or competition.

The World War I Victory Medal, created in 1919 separately by both the Army and the Navy, was awarded to any service member who served in any military capacity during the U.S. involvement in World War I and also to those involved in the following years

APPENDIX

in military operations in European Russia and Siberia in the wake of the Russian October Revolution. Since these medals were created after the end of the war, they were mailed to each serviceman. They were accompanied by a variety of clasps and devices which denoted citations for exceptional service and the battles in which each soldier was involved. The medal was bronze with winged Victoria, the Roman personification of Victory, holding a sword and shield on the front. On the back across the top is carved "The Great War for Civilization" along with stars along the bottom. In the center is a column of staves wrapped in a cord which is superimposed upon a U.S. badge. This design is surrounded by a list of the countries of the Allied forces.

Division and Unit Insignia:

The Shoulder Sleeve Insignia (SSI) Sandlin wore on his uniform is the 33rd Division Patch. Nicknames: "Illinois Division"; "Prairie Division"; "Golden Cross Division".

Activated: July 1917 (National Guard Division from Illinois). Overseas: May 1918. Major operations: Meuse-Argonne, Somme offensive. Casualties: Total 6,864 (KIA-691, WIA 6,173). Commanders: Maj. Gen. George Bell, Jr. (25 August 1917), Brig. Gen. H. D. Todd, Jr. (19 September 1917), Maj. Gen. George Bell, Jr. (7 December 1917). Returned to U.S. and inactivated: May 1919.

This was the Distinctive Unit Insignia (DUI) of the 132nd Infantry Regiment. It was approved 13 March 1925, so Willie would not have worn this item on his uniform. However, the Green Oak Tree at the top is for the Forges Wood battle and the stars represent the five major operations in which the Regiment took part in France.

1. Amiens, 17 July – 5 August 1918.
2. Somme Offensive, 8 – 20 August 1918.
3. Verdun-Frommerville, 8 – 25 September 1918.
4. Meuse-Argonne, 26 September – 21 October 1918.
5. Troyon, 25 October 1918 – 11 November 1918.

Foreign Decorations

Between July 9, 1918, the date of the approval of the act of Congress (40 Stat. L. 872) permitting members of the military forces of the United States serving in the World War to accept and wear certain foreign decorations, and the close of the last fiscal year, the various nations allied or associated with the United States during the World War awarded a total of 18,019 decorations to officers and enlisted men of the United States Army to members of American welfare organizations and to American civilians connected in some capacity with the allied armies or the several interallied commissions or who otherwise rendered meritorious services to the allied cause. The time limit prescribed in the act of Congress approved July 9, 1918, within which such decorations could be accepted by members of the military establishment expired on July 1, 1922. The statistics of these decorations, however, are undergoing constant change and revision, because of cancellations, corrections, and discoveries as to decorations awarded within the time limit but which had not previously been indexed.

France:	Military medal (medaille militaire)	304
	War Cross (croix de guerre) w/Palm	1,859
Italy:	War Cross (croce di guerra)	395
Montenegro:	Medal for military bravery (medaille pour la bravoure militaire)	94

FRANCE – The Croix de Guerre 1914–1918 (War Cross) is a French military decoration, the first version of the Croix de guerre. It was created to recognize French and allied soldiers who were cited for valorous service during World War I, similar to the British mentioned in dispatches but with multiple degrees equivalent to other nations' decorations for courage.

Soon after the outbreak of World War I, French military officials felt that a new military award had to be created. At that time, the Citation du Jour ("Daily Citation") already existed to acknowledge soldiers, but it was just a sheet of paper. Only the Médaille Militaire and Legion of Honour were bestowed for courage in the field, due to the numbers now involved, a new decoration was required in earnest. At the end of 1914, General Boëlle, Commandant in Chief of the French 4th Army Corps, tried to convince the French administration to create a formal military award. Maurice Barrès, the noted writer and parliamentarian for Paris, gave Boëlle support in his efforts.

On December 23, 1914, the French parliamentarian Georges Bonnefous proposed a legislative bill to create the Croix de la Valeur Militaire ("Cross of Military Valour")

APPENDIX

signed by 66 other parliamentarians. Émile Driant, a parliamentarian who served in the war zone during much of this time, became its natural spokesman when he returned to the legislature. On 18 January 1915, Driant submitted this bill but the name of the military award was renamed to Croix de Guerre ("War Cross"). After parliamentary discussions, the bill was adopted on 2 April 1915. World War I began in 1914 and ended in 1918, so the final name adopted is "Croix de guerre 1914–1918".

Sandlin received his medal with Bronze palm (palme de bronze): which was for those who were cited at the army level.

FRANCE – The Médaille Militaire (Military Medal) is a military decoration of the French Republic for other ranks for meritorious service and acts of bravery in action against an enemy force. It is the third highest award of the French Republic, after the Légion d'honneur, a civil and military order, and the Ordre de la Libération, a second world war-only order. The Médaille militaire is therefore the most senior entirely military active French decoration.

The award was first established in 1852 by the first President of the French Republic, Louis-Napoléon Bonaparte who may have taken his inspiration from a medal established and awarded by his father, Louis Bonaparte, King of Holland.

ITALY – The Croce al Merito di Guerra (War Merit Cross) was awarded to members of the armed forces for war merit in operations on land, sea or in the air, after minimum one year of service in the trenches or elsewhere, in contact with an enemy. This bronze cross was instituted by King Victor Emanuel III on 19 January 1918 and was also awarded to those who, wounded in combat, were given the Medal of the Wounded or to those who, mentioned for war merit, received a promotion. When having performed an act of valor which was deemed insufficient for the Medal of Military Valor, the War Merit Cross could be awarded instead.

The reverse bears a 5-pointed star on a background of rays. The obverse has the royal cypher in the upper arm (VE III under a crown), "MERITO DI GVERRA" (War Merit) on the horizontal arms and a roman sword point upwards, on oak leaves, in the lower arm. Sandlin did not receive this medal until 1921.

MONTENEGRO – The Medal for Military Bravery (Medaille pour la Bravoure Militaire) was created in 1841 and remained in use until 1919, the end of independent Montenegro. Until 1895, the medal was hung from a ribbon with the Montenegrin colors of red, white, and blue. From 1895 onwards, the ribbon became white with red edges. This medal was awarded to officers and soldiers and officers for acts of brav-

SERGEANT SANDLIN

ery and was second only to the Milosh Obilich Medal, the highest Montenegrin military decoration.

[from the ANNUAL REPORT OF THE SECRETARY OF WAR TO THE PRESIDENT WAR DEPARTMENT FISCAL YEAR ENDED JUNE 30, 1923 (Washington: Government Printing Office, 1923), pages 162-174]

For Italian Cross: See *Lexington Leader*, 18 December 1921,

APPENDIX B

Thousandsticks, Hyden. June 16, 1949.

Resolutions

WHEREAS, on Sunday, May 29th, 1949, our beloved and most faithful comrade, Willie Sandlin answered his last Roll Call on earth and joined other comrades in that place set apart to the real veterans who have fought to keep our country free.

Willie Sandlin enlisted in the Regular Army April 17, 1913, served on the Mexican Border in 1916; served overseas with the 33rd Division in France; was one of the few to be awarded the Congressional Medal of Honor for his unsurpassed feat of killing twenty-four Germans single handed in one day, and, according to the official record, of all men who were awarded such a medal, he was the greatest of all. He was known as the most modest hero of the First World War, and consistently, to the last, refused to accept many lucrative offers to commercialize on his deeds as a soldier.

He returned home on July third, 1924 became a member of Hugh McKee Post No. 677, Veterans of Foreign Wars, the oldest Post in Kentucky, and also known throughout the United States as having more decorated veterans as members than any other Post in the National Organization. He served as Chief of Staff for the Department of Kentucky a number of terms and at the time of his death had served for over twenty years as Aide-de-Camp to the Commander-in-Chief, Medal of Honor Class. He represented the Post at National Conventions throughout the country for several years, and brought not only to his Post, but to all Kentucky, more honor and renoun (sic) than any single man for many years.

NOW, BE IT RESOLVED: by Hugh-McKee Post 677, Lexington, Kentucky, that this Post has lost its most valuable member, and the most decarated [sic] one, as well as one of the best workers; that a copy of this Resolution be spread upon the Minutes of the Post; a copy to his family; to Foreign Service, and to the two Lexington newspapers, the Louisville, Kentucky papers, and the newspaper at Hyden, Kentucky, and that the Charter of the Post be draped for thirty days.

> R. E. Lee Murphy, Past
> Department Commander
> Taylor H. House
> Past Commander
> Kelly S. Rogers, Member
> Of Committee

SERGEANT SANDLIN

Resolutions

In memory of our departed brother Willie Sandlin, who departed this life May 29, 1949.

Whereas, It has pleased the Grand Master of the Universe in his infinite wisdom and knowledge to call from labor here on earth to everlasting refreshment in that Celestial Lodge on High the soul of beloved Bro. Willie Sandlin, therefore be it

Resolved, That the fraternity has lost a true and faithful brother, our Nation one of its most illustrous [sic] heroes and the family a devoted and loving husband and father, be it

Resolved, By Hyden Lodge No. 664, F. & M. that we offer our deepest and most sincere sympathy to his loved ones and commend them to our Heavenly Father who doeth all things well, and be it further

Rsolved [sic], That a copy of these resolutions be spread on the minutes of this lodge as a permanent memorial to our deceased brother, that a copy be sent to the bereaved family, a copy be sent to the press and the Masonic Home Journal for publication.

    Edward N. Farmer
    Curt Wooton
    Nick Lewis, Jr.
    Committee

Card Of Thanks

    The family of Sgt. Willie Sandlin wishes to express their grateful appreciation to their friends and neighbors for their kindness and sympathy during the illness and death of their beloved husband and father. They also wish to thank the Rev. Benton P. Deaton for the kind way in which he conducted the funeral services, and those who rendered special music. The American Legion, The Masonic Lodge, and the Hyden Funeral Home for the efficient way in which they conducted the funeral and burial arrangements. For the many and beautiful floral tributes we are also deeply grateful.

    Mrs. Belvia Sandlin
    Mrs. Vorres Day
    Mrs. Leona Asher
    Mrs. Nancy Ruth Asher
    Mrs. Florence Asher
    Robert E. Lee Sandlin

APPENDIX C
Recipients of the Medal of Honor From Kentucky

Civil War 1861-1865
Army Captain William P. Black
Army Private John H. Callahan
Army Sergeant John S. Darrough
Army Private John Davis
Army Drummer William H. Horsfall
Army Private Aaron Hudson
Army Private Henry B. Mattingly
Army Sergeant Francis M. McMillen
Navy Landsman Daniel Noble
Army Private Oliver P. Rood
Army Sergeant Andrew J. Smith
Army Private William Steinmetz
Army Doctor Mary Edwards Walker
Army Major John F. Weston
Army Colonel James A. Williamson

Indian Campaigns 1870-1891
Army Second Lieutenant Thomas Cruse
Army First Sergeant William L. Day
Army Corporal John J. Givens
Army Private William M. Harris
Army Captain John B. Kerr
Army Private Franklin M. McDonald
Army Private George D. Scott
Army Sergeant Thomas Shaw
Army Private Thomas W. Stivers
Army Private Thomas Sullivan
Army Saddler Otto E. Voit
Army Sergeant Brent Woods

Actions in Peacetime 1871-1910
Navy Seaman Edward W. Boers
Navy Watertender Edward A. Clary
Navy Quarter Gunner George Holt

SERGEANT SANDLIN

Wars of American Expansion 1897-1902
Army Colonel J. Franklin Bell
Army First Lieutenant Benjamin F. Hardaway
Army Private James J. Nash

World War I 1917-1918
Army Sergeant Willie Sandlin

World War II 1941-1945
Marine Corps Corporal Richard E. Bush
Army Technical Sergeant Morris E. Crain
Marine Corps Private First Class Leonard F. Mason
Marine Corps Reserve Private First Class Wesley Phelps
Army Private Wilburn K. Ross
Marine Corps Private First Class Luther Skaggs, Jr.
Army Staff Sergeant Junior J. Spurrier
Army Sergeant John C. Squires

Korean War 1950-1953
Marine Corps Captain William E. Barber
Marine Corps Private First Class William B. Baugh
Army Corporal John J. Collier
Army First Lieutenant Carl H. Dodd
Army Second Lieutenant Darwin K. Lyle
Army Private First Class David M. Smith
Army Private First Class Ernest E. West

Vietnam War 1961-1975
Army Sergeant Charles E. Fleek
Army Staff Sergeant Don Jenkins
Army Private First Class Billy L. Lauffer
Army Sergeant First Class Gary L. Littrell
Army Second Lieutenant John J. McGinty, III
Army Private First Class David P. Nash
Marine Corps Lance Corporal Joe C. Paul

Operation Enduring Freedom 2001-Present
Marine Corps Sergeant Dakota Meyer

INDEX

Sergeant Sandlin: Kentucky's Forgotten Hero
Proper Name Index

A

Abner, Bill 37
Adams, Benjamin 233
Adkinson, Kandie 236
Allen, Paula 236
Antin, Lucile Louise 124
Arnold, Sarah 175
Asher, Butch 12
Asher, Chad 232
Asher, Gary Ray 232
Asher, George 205
Asher, J. H. 117
Asher, Jamie Karl 232
Asher, Kim Yvette 232
Asher, Michelle Tina 232
Asher, William Dillon 232

B

Bailey, Sherrill Lynn 232
Baker, Ance 99
Baker, Eliza 36
Baker, James Todd 36
Baker, Newton 28, 84
Baldwin, Yvonne 107, 111
Barger, Harrison 33
Barlow, Oliver K. 95
Bartlett, Jennifer 236
Begley, Boone 193
Begley, M.C. 184, 186
Beshear, Steve 216

Bettez, David L. 27, 238
Beverly, Arthur 51
Blankenship, Diane 236
Bowling, Stephen 33, 35, 236
Bowman, Walter 236
Breckinridge, Mary C. 102, 103, 104, 105, 106
Brett, Lloyd M. 95
Brewer, Nancy Ruth Sandlin 87, 88, 166, 172, 200, 219, 225, 231, 232, 264
Brewer, Patricia Ann 232
Brock, Hiram 135-137, 179
Bustetter, Debbie 238
Byers, Lila 172
Byers, Mabel 172

C

Campbell, William 101
Cantwell, Laurie 238
Carroll, Julian 213, 214
Catton, Bruce 92
Clarke, Leif 236
Cobb, Irving S. 126
Collier, S. R. 28
Cook, Sophia Roberts 197
Coolidge, Calvin 95, 96, 122
Cooper, Gary 21
Cosper, Debbie 236
Crabbe, John G. 23
Creech, Jesse O. 95

SERGEANT SANDLIN

D
Day, Gloria Jean 232
Day, John F. 197
Day, Lloyd 232
Day, Vorres Sandlin 87, 88, 113, 151, 157, 166, 173, 200, 219, 225, 227, 230, 232, 264
Day, Willie Sandlin 230, 232
Deaton, Benton P. 211
Deffinger, Carol Lee 232
Dell, Jessie 84
Duffield, William 28

E
Eisenhower, Dwight D. 140
Evans, Joe 21
Eversole, J. B. 95, 117, 182

F
Farmer, Edward N. 264
Fetner, Claiborne 117
Fields, J. W. 94
Flagg, James Montgomery 30
Flaherty, Jason 236
Ford, Wendell 213, 214, 27
Fox, Herman H. 181, 183
Freeman, George 183

G
Gabbard, J. K. 99
Gabbard, Mrs. Doshia 207
Giddings, Anna 172
Gifford, Dan 8, 9, 238
Gilley, Charles 8, 9, 236, 238
Gilley, Peggy 236
Gilligan, Michael B. 183
Goebel, William 23
Griffith, D. W. 126

H
Haga, Donna Gail 232
Hamby, Terry 233
Hamilton, Clifford 236
Hamrick, Leona 236
Hardin, Phil 52
Hart, Joe 37, 47
Head, Joseph B. 95, 182
Herzinger, Kyna 236
Hines, Frank T. 130
Hitler, Adolph 190
Holbrook, Allison 236
Hoover, Herbert 140-141
House, Taylor H. 263
Huff, Ray 204
Hunt, Sam 99
Huston, Ruth 105, 172
Hutchins, J. W. 106
Hyden, John 169

J
Jones, Arthur 81
Jones, James 81
Jones, Loyd 101
Joseph, Samuel 92, 93

K
Kersey, Eleanor 236
Kettel, Jim 236
Kidwell, Judith 235, 236
Kirk, Wilbur 227
Kooser, John 162

L
Leming, Buzzy 10
Leming, Carl 8, 9, 10, 238
Leslie, Preston, H. 169
Lewis, Drucilla 173

INDEX

Lewis, Nick 263
Lewis, W. H. 80

M

MacArthur, Douglas 140
MacKenzie, Sir Leslie 105, 106
Maggard, G. G. 175
Mancy, Allan 37
Martin, George B. 28
Mason, Richard J., Jr. 222
McDaniel, Kim 236
McDonald, Sharon 236
McKee, Mrs. 173
McVey, Frank L. 178
Morris, "Merdie" 198
Morrow, Edwin P. 84
Mulligan, James Hillary 202, 203
Muncy, Florence Sandlin 11, 16, 37, 79, 87, 88, 90, 101, 106, 114, 150-158, 162, 164, 198, 200, 213, 219, 225, 227, 228, 231, 232, 234, 238, 264
Muncy, J. M. 175
Muncy, Vidge 37
Murphy, Robert E. Lee 94, 95, 97, 98, 123-130, 133, 182, 183, 263

N

Nantz, Mrs. Cal 197
Napier, Mrs. Clark 193
Newton, Patricia Ann 232
Nicholls, Lew
Nichols, George R. 231
Nichols, Leona Sandlin 11, 12, 86, 87, 88, 107, 157, 158, 163, 165-166, 200, 205, 219, 225, 228, 230, 232, 234, 264
Norwood, Florence 16, 79

O

Onkst, Wayne 212, 236, 238
Osborne, Don 236

P

Patterson, Jennifer 236
Patton, George S. 45, 140
Peabody, Lue 200, 232, 234
Pendarvis, Edwina 167, 235, 238
Perkins, Carl D. 213, 214
Perry, Julianne 236
Pershing, John J. 37, 43, 44, 45, 48, 53, 56, 57, 58, 59, 60, 61, 62, 79, 95, 96, 252
Powers, Jim 236
Purcell, Amy 236

R

Rayburn, Sam 21
Rich, S. H. 99
Roark, F. M. 126, 131
Roberts, Golden 195, 197
Roberts, James 236
Roberts, Ottis 197
Roberts, Sally Ann 154-155, 158, 197, 211, 236
Roberts, Watt 195, 197
Roberts, William B. 86, 89, 90, 151, 154, 155, 163, 175, 196, 197, 211, 236
Robinson, Carolyn Denise 232
Rogers, Harry L. 84
Rogers, James E. 222
Rogers, Kelly S. 263
Rogers, Will 142
Roosevelt, Franklin D. 140-142, 190, 192, 193, 198
Roosevelt, Theodore 43

S
Samson, Flem D. 133, 187
Sandlin, Charlie 33, 36, 81, 99, 207
Sandlin, Cora 87, 88, 113, 157, 183, 211, 228
Sandlin, Elihu 32, 36, 81, 99
Sandlin, John 32, 33, 34, 35, 36, 81, 207
Sandlin, Lucinda Abner 32, 33, 34, 35, 36
Sandlin, Margaret Marie Butler 231, 232
Sandlin, Mathew 33, 36, 81, 207
Sandlin, Phillip Douglas 232
Sandlin, Robert E. Lee 87, 88, 153, 157-158, 164, 182, 219, 225, 227, 231, 232, 264
Sandlin, Rose 87, 88, 211, 228
Sandlin, Timothy Robert 232
Shell, "Uncle John" 93
Sizemore, Maggie 175
Slattery, Thomas O. 39
Stanly, Augustus O. 28
Stepp, Jim 236
Stewart, Cora Wilson 103, 107, 108, 109, 110, 111, 112, 113, 114, 126, 163, 180, 181, 182
Still, James 201
Story, James D. 126
Stover, Fred B. 99
Stover, J. W. 94
Street, John, 236
Street, Shelby 235, 236, 237
Sullinger, Leota 193
Sweikel, John 183
Symonds, F. C. 195

T
Terry, Elmer J. 186
Thompson, Lisa 236
Trowbridge, John 50, 223, 224, 227, 234, 236, 237

U
Ullrich, Dieter C. 236

V
VanKirk, Adam 2, 61, 236, 237, 238
Villa, Pancho 43, 44, 48

W
Wade, Leigh 123
Walker, John W. 99
Weddington, Daniel 236
Wellman, Billy G. 227, 228
Werner, Marcy 236
Whalen, Debbie 236
Whiting, N. E. 187
Whitney, Nathaniel E. 182
Williams, Gracie 18
Wilson, Caroline 236
Wilson, Woodrow 24, 26, 31, 43
Wolf, E. B. 110
Woodfill, Samuel 94, 95, 96, 97, 98, 133
Wooton, Kurt 263
Wooton, Mary 86, 234

Y
Yeager, Addie Mae 110
York, Alvin 14, 16, 17, 19, 20, 21, 93, 100, 114, 117, 133, 134

ABOUT THE AUTHOR

James M. Gifford is the CEO & Senior Editor of the Jesse Stuart Foundation, a regional press and bookseller headquartered in Ashland, Kentucky. During his thirty-three years at the helm of the Foundation, Gifford has edited and published 150 books that focus on the history and literature of Kentucky and Appalachia. Dr. Gifford received the B.A. degree from Maryville College, the M.A. degree from Middle Tennessee State University, and his Ph.D. in history from the University of Georgia. He has published in national historical and literary journals, along with numerous articles and essays in state journals, magazines, and newspapers. Dr. Gifford has won professional awards as a teacher, author, and publisher. His *Jesse Stuart: An Extraordinary Life* was nominated for the Weatherford Award in 2010.

ABOUT THE DESIGNER

Adam VanKirk is the owner of Right Eye Graphics, a digital and print marketing agency in Ashland, Kentucky. He spent 20 years in newspaper journalism, working in editorial design and management for three daily publishers in Kentucky, Ohio and West Virginia. He has been recognized for his work with dozens of individual and collaborative awards by the Kentucky Press Association. VanKirk's design work with *Jesse Stuart: Immortal Kentuckian* led to the 2016 Award of Excellence: Hard Cover in the Southeastern Library Association Southern Books Competition. He received a KPA 1st place award for Best Graphic in Kentucky's largest newspaper category in 2016. Right Eye Graphics was a 2017 Northeast Kentucky Small Business Awards nominee for Service Business of the Year.

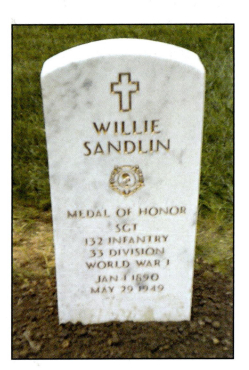